How to Write a Non-fiction Book in 60 Days

Paul Lima

Published by
Five Rivers Chapmanry
www.5rivers.org

Leeds Metropolitan University

Published by Five Rivers Chapmanry www.5rivers.org
Manufactured in the U.S.A.
Published in Canada

Second Edition 2008

Library & Archives Canada/Bibliothèque & Archives Canada Data Main entry under title:

How to Write a Non-fiction Book in 60 Days
Lima, Paul

ISBN 978-0-9739278-4-9

1. Title

Also by Paul Lima

Everything You Wanted to Know About Freelance Writing...

The Six-Figure Freelancer: How to Find, Price and Manage Corporate Writing Assignments

Business of Freelance Writing: How to Develop Article Ideas and Sell Them to Newspapers and Magazines\

Copywriting That Works: Bright ideas to Help You Inform, Persuade, Motivate and Sell!

How to Write Media Releases to Promote Your Business, Organization or Event

Do you Know Where Your Website Ranks? How to Optimize Your Website for the Best Possible Search Engine Results

Build A Better Business Foundation: Create a Business Vision, Write a Business Plan, Produce a Marketing Plan.

If You Don't Know Where You are Going, How are You Going to Get There? Business Vision Short eReport

Building Your Business Plan and Your Marketing Plan: A Step-By-Step Guide to Planning & Promoting Your Business Short eReport

Put Time On Your Side: Time Management Short eReport.

Available through www.paullima.com/books

Acknowledgements

I would like to thank freelance writer/editor Angie Gallop (www.angiegallop.com) for her help in editing this book. Her comments were most insightful. In addition, I'd like to thank Lorina Stephens of Five Rivers Chapmanry (www.5rivers.org) for encouraging me to take a popular print-on-demand book to the next level – making it available to a broader audience through a variety of distribution channels.

I wrote this book because I kept on running into budding authors who could tell me about their great book ideas but somehow were not able to actually write their books. When I told them that I had written 10 books and major reports and two comprehensive university course curriculums (*Copywriting that Works* and *The Business Approach to Writing*) in under five years, and had written the first draft of each project in about two months, they thought I was telling tall tales. So I set out to show potential authors how they could do what I have done several times over.

You are looking at the result of my work – *How to Write a Non-fiction Book in 60 Days*, written in… well, 60 days. If I can do it, you can too. I have no super powers; however, I have a method that helps me get organized before I write, and that helps me write efficiently and, I would like to believe, effectively. If you want to find out how to do it, read on… All the best with your writing!

Paul Lima

What does it take to write a book in 60 days?

It takes an idea.

How to Write a Non-Fiction Book in 60 Days spells out in detail the process required to move from your idea to a solid first draft of your book — in 60 days.

It takes purpose.

How to Write a Non-Fiction Book in 60 Days will help you clearly define your purpose so you can focus on achieving what you set out to do.

It takes knowledge of your reader.

How to Write a Non-Fiction Book in 60 Days will help you ascertain what your readers know, and what they need to know, so you can logically present the information required to meet their expectations.

It takes time.

How to Write a Non-Fiction Book in 60 Days will show you how to use your time productively to brainstorm all you need to know about your subject matter, to organize your thoughts and to outline your book before you write. And it will show you how to write effectively and efficiently from outline point to outline point, until you complete a solid first draft of your book — in 60 working days.

Table of Contents

Introduction

Welcome to *How to Write a Non-Fiction Book in 60 Days*, a book written specifically for non-fiction authors who have great ideas for books but are not sure how to turn their ideas into books. *How to Write a Non-Fiction Book in 60 Days* is for you:

- if you give speeches or conduct seminars and want to write a book to complement your public speaking;
- if you teach a college or university course or conduct training and want to write a textbook or extended training manual;
- if you have a unique take on an issue or if you support a particular cause and want to inform others about your point of view;
- if you want to write your autobiography or family history or tell a compelling story based on your life experiences or interests;
- if you want to write a solid draft of a non-fiction book in 60 days.

How to Write a Non-Fiction Book in 60 Days will show you how to brainstorm your subject matter to get down on paper all you need to address in your book. It will show you how to organize and outline your thoughts. And it will show you how to write efficiently and effectively from outline point to outline point so you can produce a solid first draft of your book in 60 days.

How to Write a Non-Fiction Book in 60 Days gives you peer-editing and self-editing hints and tips. It includes a chapter on how to construct sentences and structure paragraphs, for readers who are not completely confident in their ability to write. Any author who wants to self-publish will find the chapter on self-publishing and print-on-demand of particular interest.

Unlike many other self-help books, *How to Write a Non-Fiction Book in 60 Days* makes no outlandish promises of riches or mega-success, other than to say that you will produce a solid first draft of your book if you devote about four hours a day over 60 working days to the process outlined here.

If you feel like you've been spinning your wheels, this book will get you grounded and focused. It will show you how to turn your idea into a book — in 60 days, which is what I presume you want to do because you have purchased a book entitled *How to Write a Non-Fiction Book in 60 Days.*

Chapter 1: Can You Write A Book In 60 Days?

Is it possible to write a book in 60 days? Yes. I am living proof. I have written 11 books and short reports — each in less than 60 days. Many other writers I know have written books in under 60 days too. It can be done. It is being done. You can do it. This book will show you how to do it.

When it comes to writing a book in 60 days there are a couple of caveats, as you might expect. The first caveat: the process outlined in this book focuses on writing non-fiction. That is not to say you can't write a novel in 60 days. However, the process would be somewhat different from the one explained here. The next caveat is that I presume you have an idea for your book and are a subject expert or have acquired the information and knowledge you need to write your book. In other words, the 60 days does not include time spent on research or conducting interviews.

That said, you don't spend the 60 days focused exclusively on writing the book either, at least not in the conventional sense of writing. Built into the 60 days is time to do the following:

- Think about your subject matter and your purpose.
- Determine how best to convey the information required to achieve your purpose.
- Identify what your readers already know and need to know.

- Organize and outline your book, which is crucial to the writing process.
- Write your first draft.

Notice I said first draft. In other words, the process I am going to explain here does not include (much) editing or proofreading. If you follow the process, you will write a solid, well-structured, comprehensive first draft. You will be able to conduct a final edit or send it to an editor for comments and proofreading. Then you can shop your book around to an agent or publisher or self-publish it.

You need the Three D's

Just what does it take to complete a non-fiction book in 60 days? It takes subject knowledge, of course. It takes the ability to write, but you don't have to be a professional writer. Finally, it takes the Three D's: *Desire*, *Discipline* and *Dedication*.

The fact that you have purchased this book demonstrates desire: you want to write a book. Good start. This book spells out a process and explains why you should follow it and it establishes a timetable, or the discipline, required to complete your book in 60 days. It is, of course, up to you to spend the time required to write your book. In other words, you have to dedicate the time required to complete your book.

Do you have to dedicate time each day for the next 60 days? Not at all. The time you spend depends on your schedule. If you can only work on your book one day a week, you can spread your 60 days over the next 60 weeks. If you can work on the book a couple days a week, you can complete the book in about 30 weeks. If you can work on the book every day, you can complete a solid first draft in 60 days.

With that in mind, let's think about time. I suggest you write down how you are going to spend your time on your book and then commit to it. Create your version of the sentence below. Write it down. Post it where you can see it.

> I will work on my book [every day, every Saturday, two days a week...] until I complete a solid first draft.

Working on the book does not mean sitting in front of the computer ruminating. It means diligently applying the principles and techniques described in this book. In short, if you want to turn your desire into reality, dedicate time in a disciplined manner to your book-writing project.

Does that sound like work?

It is work. Books do not write themselves. However, I am going to show you how to get to the point where you can say, "It's all over but the writing." Trust me, that is a wonderful place to be. Then I am going to show you how to write your book in short bursts or a series of focused chunks — section by section, or chapter by chapter — until it is all over.

Writing any book is not easy. But if you follow the process outlined here, writing your book is going to be one heck of a lot easier than sitting down in front of a blank screen and pounding on the keyboard, hoping to fill the screen with something that resembles a book.

Are you ready? If so, let's begin!

Chapter 2: The Journey Begins: Day 1

Look at your calendar. You have started your 60-day journey.

Before we do any writing, I want you to do some reading. Just so you don't think I am making you consume time that is not part of your 60 days, notice "Day 1" is included in the title of this section. The clock is ticking. This doesn't mean you have to speed read. It just means you won't be doing any writing today. And that's okay.

As a writer, one of the most important things you can do, besides writing, is reading. But, what do you read and why? You read other books that are in the same genre as yours. Say you want to write romance for instance. You would read other romance novels to see how successful romance novelists have tackled the genre — how they hooked the reader at the beginning of the book, developed the plot and characters, held the reader's interest and reached the climax in a way that left the reader feeling satisfied.

You are reading a book entitled *How to Write a Non-Fiction Book in 60 Days*. Part of your pre-writing work is to read — or at least scan — several other non-fiction books. Over the first 30 days you spend working on your book, read at least three other books that are, in some way, related to what you want to write.

If you want to write a business book, read several business books. If you want to write a health and nutrition book, read a couple of health and nutrition books. If you want to write a bicycle repair guide, read other repair guides. Find out what works and what does not work in terms of structure, how ideas are conveyed, the actual writing and so on.

For instance, you want your book to be as well structured as possible. You want the various sections to flow in a logical manner, which can be hard to accomplish if you have never written a book before. While I am going to help you set up your book so it flows in a logical manner, it doesn't hurt to see how other authors have structured their books.

If your book is well structured and if the content flows in a logical manner, you create less work for your editor. The editor can focus on catching the little mistakes that plague us all, instead of reworking entire sections of the book (more on editing later). First, of course, you have to write your book. And while you are preparing to do that, over the next 30 days, spend some time reading and learning from other books.

Define a Non-fiction Book

Before you start to write your book, allow me to set the stage. We'll start by defining a non-fiction book, then look at elements of the non-fiction book.

There are two parts to the definition of a non-fiction book: non-fiction and book. What you are reading here is a work of non-fiction. (Although if you don't believe anyone can write a book in 60 days, you might think it's a work of fiction.)

A work of non-fiction can be defined as "true stories or books of facts and ideas." In other words, non-fiction presents factual information about real people, events, things, ideas, methods, systems or techniques. Poetry and plays can also be considered non-fiction; however, for the sake of this book, we are going to exclude them.

If you are like most non-fiction writers, you have a great interest, passion even, in a particular subject matter. It could be a business or health topic. It could be a political or cultural topic. It could relate to events pertaining to you or your family. Whatever your topic, you have experienced it as part of your life — through your education, work, business experience or through the sheer fact of living. And now you want to write a book about your knowledge or experience.

But what is a Book?

Just what is it you want to write? Go to a library or bookstore and you will see thousands of books. They are written works or compositions that have been published on bound pages. These days, they are also available in electronic format. In terms of words or pages, I've read definitions that state a book is "a publication of 49 or more pages that is not a magazine or newspaper article." Although over 49 pages, this book could be considered a booklet. Ultimately, you decide if you are writing a book, but you also have to meet your reader's expectations — for the most part, that would be 50 or more pages. For the sake of this book, I am going to presume you are writing something more substantial — 100 or more pages. However, if you are writing something shorter, continue to read. All the principles described here apply, and you will probably complete your book in less than 60 days.

A non-fiction book is generally broken down into chapters. I am going to suggest that when you hit 25,000 or more words divided into 10 or more chapters, you have a substantial non-fiction book. You can write fewer or more words. You can have fewer or more chapters. The most important thing is that you are writing about a particular topic in detail and in chapters.

We can quibble, if we want, over exact word count and number of chapters, but I think you get my drift. You are going to produce a whole lot of words on a topic of great interest to you (and, you hope, to many others) and you are going to call it a book — your book!

Elements of a Non-fiction Book

Before you write, get organized. This book will show you how to organize yourself so you can use your time productively over the 60 days. Before we get into the details, let's get mentally organized by figuring out the standard elements we will most likely cover in our book.

Perhaps the most important element of a non-fiction book, beyond the actual writing, is the subject you are writing about. Almost everything flows from it. And by everything, we mean the following elements:

- descriptive title that captures the attention of your target audience;
- dedication and/or acknowledgment(s) page;
- introduction or a foreword, which may be written by a third party and is often read by people who are thumbing through your book trying to make a buying decision;
- "about the author" section with your picture and a link to your website or your e-mail address if you want feedback;
- table of contents, which is often scanned by potential readers and, as you will see, is crucial to your writing process;
- the body of the book chunked into chapters, which reflect the table of contents;

- and, finally, perhaps a glossary, index and/or endnotes.

In short, your book does not have to include the elements of fiction, such as characters, conflict, plot, setting and a narrator. However, you might use some of those elements in examples or to demonstrate particular points. More importantly, your writing must be engaging and captivating if you want to hold your reader's interest. I don't care how important your topic is, if there is not a logical flow to your thoughts and if your writing is deadly dull or confusing, the reader will not finish your book.

If you have not done much writing, this may feel a tad intimidating. But this book will help you to get organized. The emphasis here will be to help you outline and write individual chapters. Outlining will help you bring a logical flow to your thoughts. It will break your book down into short, focused chunks you can write quickly, giving you less opportunity for writing long, off-topic digressions that tend to bore readers. However, before we plunge in and get organized, I want to introduce you to some important aspects of the writing process. Almost any successful writer knows how to harness the writing process. In addition, I am going to give you a few writing exercises you will apply over your 60 days.

If you are thinking all this is going to take some time, you are right. If you are thinking that I am cheating — that this is going to make the entire process longer than 60 days — you are wrong. I am going to let you take a couple of days to do some pre-writing exercises and to learn about some of the tools we'll be incorporating into the writing process. So the clock is ticking; you will be moving forward even as you spend time picking up a bit of theory and doing the exercises presented here.

One More Note about Your 60 Days

People often ask me if I am talking about 24-hour days. No, absolutely not. They often ask if they have to work full time at writing their book over 60 days, say 8 to 10 hours a day. Again, my answer is no.

You can do what I am suggesting here by working about four hours per day for 60 days. Some days you may put in more time. Other days you may put in less time. If you can only afford an hour or two per day, the entire process might take you a bit longer than 60 days, which is to be expected. At the same time, it is not really how many hours you sit in front of your computer that counts. What you do during those hours is what will enable you to write your book in 60 working days — days you spend following and applying the process detailed in this book.

Again, depending on how much time per working day you can apply to the process, it might take you more than 60 days to write your book. However, you might also complete your first draft in less time.

Note: Since it might take you more or less than 60 days to write your book, why did I use "60 days" in the title of my book? Just as you need a sexy title for your book, I needed one too. Somehow, *How to Write a Non-fiction Book in About 60 Working Days, More or Less, Depending on How Much Time per Day You Can Devote to the Project* just didn't cut it.

With that in mind, do you have a sexy title, or at least a working title, for your book? If not, take the rest of the time you have to devote to your book today and jot down some title ideas. See if you can get down a couple of ideas that will reflect what your book is about and why it will appeal to potential readers. You can revise the title later, when you complete your book. In fact, if you are like me, you will revise your title several times before you come up with one that feels right.

On the other hand, if you already have a title for your book, take the rest of the day off!

Chapter 3: Pre-Writing Exercises: Day 2

I am giving you two days of pre-writing exercises — Days 2 and 3. If you have time to spare, you might be able to get through these two chapters in a day. However, take time to absorb the material. And please, do the exercises. The work you do here will pay off later, when you are getting down to brass tacks.

If you are like me, you fear the blank screen or blank page. You look at it and feel intimidated. You see it as an empty vessel you have to fill with wonderful words — only you are not sure which words to use, the order in which to use them or how to use all those squiggles known as punctuation marks.

Perhaps you are not like me. Perhaps you love the sight of a blank page. You view it as a blank canvas, an opportunity to create. However, you may feel your creations take too long to come to fruition. You start. You stop. You start again. Moving forward is a slow, painful journey, and you often don't seem to reach your destination. Seldom do you produce work that is satisfactory. All I can say is…

Welcome to the World of Writing

English is a convoluted and inconsistent language. That in itself can be frustrating. Like me, you may also have some early memories of schoolteachers who seemed to relish slashing thick red marks through your earnest writing efforts, leaving you intimidated by the act of writing.

I want to help you relax a bit. I want you to understand that making so-called mistakes is simply a part of the writing process, which we will look at in detail later. Grammar and spelling count, to be sure, but mistakes can be caught and corrected by an editor or proof-reader. What is most important, when it comes to writing, is how you convey your ideas. If you try to catch the little mistakes as you write, you will let grammar and spelling distract you from the job of writing. You will lose your train of thought and you will write in an inefficient and ineffective manner. The writer and the editor should be kept separate. In short, when it comes to writing, it is your job to write. When you have finished a section or chapter — or even your book — you can edit and correct.

I will soon introduce you to two writing exercises — freefall and directed freefall. They will help you separate the writer you are from the editor you need to be later in the process. The writer is your creative self and exists on the right side of your brain. The editor is your logical or linear self and exists on the left side of the brain. To separate writer from editor, your goal is to write first, revise later. Doing so keeps the left and right sides of your brain separated, as it were. Ironically, this makes you a better writer and a better editor.

The Internal Critic

We all have an internal critic harping at us to get our writing right. At the same time, it is just so darn difficult to remember all the minor and inconsistent rules of English.

My internal critic is Mr. C, my grade five teacher. Mr. C took his government-appointed task of teaching me perfect spelling and grammar very seriously. Wielding his red marker like the sword of

Zorro, he forcefully cut huge red gashes across my mistakes. He never once commented on content or creativity. There was no room for art or craft. To him, writing was all about correct spelling, grammar and neatness or penmanship, as it was called.

In grade five, as our spelling and penmanship improved, Mr. C's students were supposed to graduate from pencil to pen. But Mr. C made me use a pencil all year because I could not spell well or write neatly. I only received my pen on the last day of class. Mr. C tossed it at me and said, "Here, Lima, you'll need this next year. Good luck!"

But look at the language I was trying to master! We have this so-called rule, "i" before "e" except after "c". But how do you spell "weird"? That word is just, well, plain weird.

Mr. C was right. My writing was messy. For whatever reason, I could not remember most of the rules of spelling and grammar. And when I did manage to remember some of them, I could not remember the exceptions. Bottom line, I was a poor speller and I did not punctuate very well. When you can't spell well, you learn how to hide the fact, which is why my penmanship was so poor. When you don't know if it's "i" before "e", you make a chubby "i" and a skinny "e" and put the dot right in the middle — hoping to fool the teacher!

I battle Mr. C whenever I sit down to write. However, I have been earning my living as a professional writer for over 25 years and am the author of several books on business writing and the business of freelance writing (www.paullima.com/books). Today, when Mr. C rears his fearsome head, I say, "Get thee behind me!" and I keep on writing. I write through typos and grammatical errors. Through incomplete sentences and incorrect words. I write until I have finished an error-filled first draft, and I laugh in his face. Because I have learned something about writing. Writing is a process in which the act of writing is separate from the act of editing.

Mr. C wasn't teaching us to be good writers. He was teaching us to be good editors. But the writing has to sparkle or you will have little to feed your editor. If you do not follow the process, Mr. C will trip you up every time. He will get you revising and editing when you should be creating. He will cause you to waste time proofreading work that is not yet at the first draft stage. In other words, it is okay to make mistakes when you write because the process allows you to correct them, or pay others to do so, when you finish your first draft. After all, your first draft is for your eyes only, so who cares if it contains spelling or grammatical mistakes? You can correct them before you send it out to an agent or publisher or before you self-publish your work.

Words for Thought

Writing can be difficult enough without having your internal critic squeeze the last ounce of fun out of what should be a challenging but enjoyable and creative project. With that in mind, before we try the writing exercises, chew on a few words for thought:

"It took me my whole life to learn how to paint like a child again."
- Pablo Picasso

"Never look at a reference book while doing a first draft. You want to write a story? Fine. Put away your dictionary, your encyclopaedias, your World Almanac and your thesaurus.... You think you might have misspelled a word? Okay, so here's your choice: either look it up in the dictionary to make sure you have it right — and break your train of thought — or spell it phonetically and correct it later. Why not? Do you think the word is going to go away? When you sit down to write, write. Don't do anything else except go to the bathroom and only do that if it absolutely cannot be put off."
- Stephen King

So what are Picasso and King saying? When you are writing (or engaged in any creative act, such as painting), you must overcome your inhibitions and internal censors. In short, when you are writing, spelling and grammar do not count. There will be time for those adult tasks — editing, proofreading and correcting — later, once you have fun and complete your first draft.

Spell-check and Grammar-check Off

If you are using a word processing program like Microsoft Word and you have your spell checker and grammar checker turned on, you are inviting Mr. C to inhibit your writing. The green and red squiggles under your words, phrases and sentences mean you are seeing (and correcting) so-called mistakes as you write — before you complete your first draft.

Every time you revise, when you should be writing, you are wasting time and derailing your train of thought. If you want to improve your writing productivity immediately, turn off spell check and grammar check and get writing.

I want to reinforce one point before we move on. Spelling and grammar are important. I try my darndest to catch spelling and grammar mistakes. I just don't do it while I am writing my first draft. After I have completed what I consider a decent first or second draft, I focus on the more mundane, yet important, task of checking spelling and grammar.

Now, let's get ready to have some fun … I mean, *write*!

Writing Exercise: Freefall

Freefall, also known as stream of consciousness, is a means of writing whereby you literally write without stopping for five minutes or more. Think of yourself as an artist practicing gesture sketching (rapidly drawing lines or "gestures" that do not necessarily become pictures, but enable the artist to play and experiment with lines he or she might later incorporate in pictures).

You don't have to have anything in particular to write about. You just put pen to paper, which is recommended over fingers to keyboard here, and write, write, write... You don't stop... No matter what. You tap into your stream of consciousness — the thoughts that are flowing through your mind. Even as you are reading this page you can hear thoughts rushing through your mind. In freefall, those thoughts are what you write... write...write.... If you feel yourself coming to a halt, doodle or use an ellipsis (...) until you tap back into the stream. Do not stop.

- Do NOT stop to correct spelling, grammar or punctuation.
- Do NOT stop to reflect upon or to edit your work.
- Do NOT stop.

It can feel unusual to write when you think you have nothing to say or to continue to write when you know you have made a typo or grammatical error, but that is the whole point. I want you to get used to the separation of writer and editor by jumping into the stream and letting the current take you somewhere, anywhere or nowhere as you write, write, write.

As you will see, freefall is a technique I will encourage you to employ after you have completed your preparation, research and organization. You'll use a version of freefall to write your book, so practice it now.

Writing this way can take a bit of getting used to, although you will probably take to it like a fish to water (or any other cliché you can think of when you are freefalling and the perfect analogy does not come immediately to mind).

I want to stress here that your freefall does not have to be a straight narrative. Have fun. Play. Push your boundaries. Do not try to impose form or narrative on your freefall; however, if you latch on to something that feels like a bit of business writing or book-related writing, run with it. Write fast. Do not pause. Especially do not pause to correct or revise.

Let's Freefall

What I suggest you do now is this: Sit comfortably where you will not be interrupted for the next while, and write for at least five or 10 minutes. Pick up your pen or pencil and start wherever you start... And don't end until you end.

If you are not ready to write, go have a cup of tea, go for a stroll, go pet your dog or cat or talk to your bird. But don't put off starting for too long. When you are ready...

Set your timer and...begin your freefall...
[Please freefall for 5 to 10 minutes before you read on.]

Freefall purpose

Now that you've done your first freefall, you may be wondering if there is a purpose to it. Is there a point or purpose to all the gesture sketching an artist does, the voice exercises an opera singer does, the stretching a runner does? Yes. This is your warm-up. This is you getting in shape. This is you learning to write for the sake of writing. This is you in a no-pressure, not-for-publication situation discovering the fun of writing, the joy of writing. This is you separating the writer from the editor. This is you learning how to become a more efficient and effective writer. This is you becoming a child again so you can paint.

Before you go on, why not try another one? Freefall for five more minutes and see where it takes you…

Directed Freefall

Directed freefall works in a manner similar to freefall, only you start with an opening line — something to kick-start your writing. Once you start, you carry on just as with freefall.

You can find directed freefall "beginnings" almost anywhere: a phrase on the radio, a sentence in the newspaper, a snippet of overheard conversation, in a book or report and so on. The first line sometimes imposes structure on a narrative passage, but not always. Sometimes it inspires focus, but not always. Sometimes it is a relief to have somewhere to start. Sometimes it makes you feel shackled. The point is to simply write no matter how you feel.

So take five to 10 minutes and try a directed freefall. If you are not ready to write, go have a cup of tea, go for a stroll, go pet your dog or cat or talk to your bird... You know the drill. If you are ready to write, start with the line below and write without stopping for at least five minutes.

> Set your timer and begin your directed freefall starting with the following line:
> *It took me a long time to...*

When you have completed your directed freefall, try several other lines. You can look for lines of your own to get you started, or you can use any of these:

- It's upsetting and frustrating when...

- If I've told you once, I've told you a thousand times...
- Terry had to reschedule the meeting because...

The goal is to see where the lines take you, to have fun, to be silly or serious, to create for the sake of creating. To write without revising. Why? Because separating the writer from the editor is an important part of the writing process. Off the top, it makes you a more efficient writer. If you work diligently at keeping the writer and editor separate, it will also make you a more effective writer.

Some people find their freefalls are little more than scattered lines but their directed freefalls seem to have more of a narrative structure. This is not the case with everyone. Some people who freefall stutter at first and then find a narrative flow. Some people who try directed freefalls find it difficult to get started because they can't relate to the opening line. However, many people who try directed freefalls discover a natural, coherent narrative flow. Having an opening line or direction can get you focused — hence a narrative develops. We will look at this later in the book; keep it in the back of your mind for now.

Before you move on, do one last thing. Count your words. How many words did you produce when freefalling? Most people find they can write 150 to 250 words in 10 minutes. Some write more; some write less.

Let's say you hit 200 words. How many words did I say there were in a book? At the bottom end, 25,000 words. At the top end for a work of non-fiction, let's say 50,000. Do the math:

$$25,000 / 200 = 125$$

What does that 125 represent? It represents the number of 10-minute chunks it will take you to write 25,000 words. In other words, 125 x 10 = 1,250 minutes or almost 21 hours.

It takes less than a day to write a 25,000-word book.

It takes less than two days to write a 50,000-word book.

Do you think I am kidding? I am not. The question you should be asking yourself is this: If it takes less than two days to write a 50,000-word book, why is this book called *How to Write a Non-Fiction Book in 60 Days?*

I told you, I needed a sexy title. I also needed one that felt credible. But the title is not a lie. Here's the secret: The time you spend not writing is just as important, perhaps even more important, than the time you spend writing. But we will get to that later.

First, however, I want you to do another writing exercise. If you have time, read on. If not, feel free to save it for the next day you work on your book.

Chapter 4: Pre-Writing Exercises: Day 3

Brainstorming and Clustering

I now want to introduce you to a brainstorming technique known as *clustering*. You will apply clustering later in this book, before you create your detailed outline and before you start to write your book, so spend some time here learning how to use this technique.

Clustering, a form of word-association or brainstorming, helps you conduct internal research before you create an outline, which you should do before you write any document — including a book.

Clustering enables you to put down on paper everything you know about and associate with a topic. It helps you get information out of your head and helps you get it down on paper, where you can see it.

In short, clustering lets you ponder a topic on paper while reducing the overall time you have to spend pondering a topic. And before you write a book, or any long document, you have to spend some ponder time.

Clustering also sparks themes and ideas related to your topic that you might not have otherwise thought up. These themes and ideas help enrich your writing, as you shall see. But what exactly is clustering? What does it look like?

Since a picture is worth a thousand words, allow me to show you an example of clustering before I describe how to engage in this activity.

The clustering example that is coming up might look like a messy web of words and phrases. It also contains gold — internal research and outline gold. You just have to learn how to extract the gold from your cluster goldmine, which I will show you how to do.

Most, but not all, of the words and phrases in your cluster threads will relate to a key word that is related to your subject or topic. In the case below, my key word was *clustering* and my topic was the process of clustering. You will see many words and phrases that do not necessarily relate to the topic of clustering.

When clustering, you put down anything that comes up, because you don't know where these word associations will lead. In other words, sometimes you have to be off-topic in order to get on-topic.

Once you have completed your clustering exercise, you can look at the words and phrases of your cluster strings rationally and separate the wheat from the chaff or the gold from the silt, so to speak. You use the wheat or the gold to create your outline, as we shall see.

Clustering Example

Take a moment to review the clustering example that follows, and read the instructions on the next page about how to cluster. Try a couple of exercises using the key words provided for you.

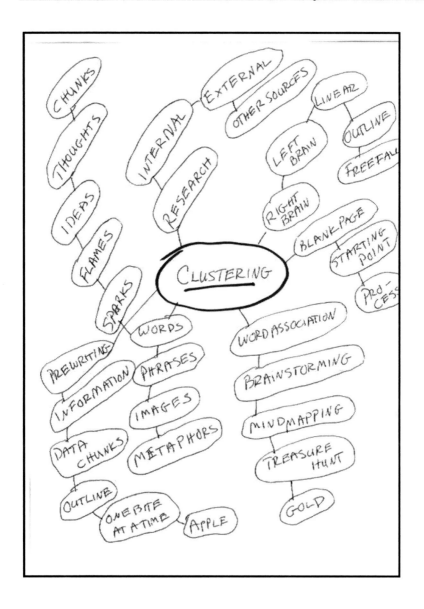

Clustering: How to Do It

When clustering, you follow a specific process in which you quickly jot down all the words and phrases you associate with a given key word or phrase. Once you are given, or decide upon, your key word or phrase you do the following:

1. Jot the key word down in the middle of a blank page; underline it and circle it.
2. Moving quickly, draw a dash from your key word and jot down the first word or phrase that comes to mind; circle the word or phrase.
3. Draw a dash from that word or phrase and jot down the next word or phrase that comes to mind.
4. Repeat until you come to the end of your word association string; you will know instinctively when this happens as you find yourself going blank.
5. Return to your key word.
6. Moving quickly, draw a new dash from your key word and jot down the next word or phrase that comes to mind; circle the word or phrase.
7. Draw a dash from that word or phrase and...continue on as described above until your mind is blank.
8. Return to your key word and continue the process.

Keep on clustering until you feel a natural end to the process, until you no longer associate any other words or phrases with your key word. You may have on the page a messy spider's web of five association strings; you may have 22 or more association strings. There is no right or wrong number.

The key is to move quickly, using the lines and circles to spark the creative side of your brain, and to cluster until you are absolutely blank.

Let's try a few exercises. And trust me on this, the work you do will pay off later.

Clustering Exercise 1

Before you complete this first exercise, read the above instructions again to make sure you understand them. Also, before clustering, loosen up on a sheet of paper by quickly drawing circles and connecting them with lines. Once you are ready, write down the key word below. Underline it and circle it. And begin.

If you are not ready, have a cup of tea, go for a stroll, go pet your dog or cat, or talk to your bird... When you are ready to begin, please use the key word:

> **HEART**
> Cluster until you run out of words or phrases you associate with heart, and then read on.
> [Please do the above exercise before you move on!]

Clustering Exercise 2

I hope you managed to fill a page with words and phrases you associate with the word *heart*. Again, the work you are doing now will pay off in spades later, so do stick with me.

Before you move on, try another exercise. If you are ready, write down the key word below and begin clustering:

APPLE
Cluster until you run out of words or phrases you
associate with apple, and then read on.
[Please do the above exercise before you move on!]

From Clustering to Outlining

Now that you've done a bit of clustering, do you have a sense of how it can help you conduct internal research and even help you produce an outline? Perhaps not yet.

So far, you have been clustering without a sense of audience or purpose. At this point, however, you should have a sense that clustering can help you produce a page full of words and phrases you associate with *heart* and with *apple*.

Imagine if you were writing about *heart* or *apple* and you had conducted some research, had an audience in mind and had a purpose you were trying to achieve. You would now have down on paper all you associate with *heart* and *apple* in relation to your research, audience and purpose.

Not every word or phrase would necessarily be applicable, but you would have many words and phrases related to your topic.

If you had completed your research or were very knowledgeable about the topic, you could take this right-brain information and separate the wheat from the chaff — literally highlight all the words and phrases you wanted to write about in your document or book.

Then you would place the relevant words or phrases in sequence — in the order in which you wanted to write about them — and produce a rough outline. After that, you would review your rough outline and revise it as required based on your purpose and your audience's needs and expectations as well as the type of and scope of the document you are producing.

In short, you would use the logical left side of your brain to work in a linear manner and produce a detailed outline based on the material served up by the creative right side of your brain.

For example, imagine if you knew a lot about producing outlines and you clustered the word *outline*. Your cluster would get all you know about the topic out of your mind and down on paper. You would then highlight the relevant information in your cluster and use it to produce an outline on the topic of *outlines*.

Once your detailed outline was complete, you would start to write. The *outline* is the magical key that will enable you to write your book in an effective yet efficient manner.

Your detailed outline of *outline* would include major topic points and minor topic (sub-topic points below each major topic point). But let me show you what I mean. Here is a major topic outline on the subject of creating outlines:

Creating Outlines
1. Define outline
2. Benefits of outlining
3. How to create an outline

With this outline in front of you, the first major topic you would write about would be the definition of an outline. The second major topic would be the benefits of outlining. Finally, you would describe how to create an outline.

However, we're not ready to write based on a major topic outline alone. Instead of simply producing a major topic outline and then writing, we would use the information in the cluster based on our key word *outline* to create a number of major topic and sub-topic points.

In other words, you would sub-divide the major topic headings into a series of minor or sub-topics as in the following example:

Creating Outlines
1. Define outline
    a. Definition of outline
    b. When to use outlines
    c. When not to use outlines
2. Benefits of outlining
    a. Provides logical structure
    b. Gives you a detailed road map
    c. Ensures all major and minor points are covered
    d. Produces greater clarity and focus
    e. Removes the stress of trying to hold on to all you know about a topic while you are writing about it
    f. Helps you detect errors in logic
    g. Allows you to write quickly in manageable chunks
    h. Ensures you do not lose your train of thought when you have to take breaks from writing
    i. Facilitates the approval process, if one is required
3. How to create an outline
    a. Pick a key word or phrase related to your topic
    b. Cluster the key word or phrase
        i. Define and describe clustering
        ii. Give a clustering exercise
        iii. Describe how to find major topic and sub-topic words and phrases in a cluster
    c. Move from clustering to linear outline
        i. Highlight relevant topic points
        ii. Outline major topic points

iii. Sub-divide topic headings where appropriate
1. Further sub-divide sub-categories if appropriate

Once you have a detailed outline in front of you, you are ready to write a series of small chunks. When you add up all the chunks, you have a comprehensive document, section, chapter or book.

If you want to write a long document, such as a book, it is unlikely you will get down every topic and sub-topic you need to include in one clustering exercise. However, later in the book, I am going to show you how to use clustering to get down on paper almost all you want to write about and how to turn that raw material into a detailed outline before you write.

By the way, some people resist clustering and outlining because they have never written that way before. I understand. I laughed when I was introduced to clustering and I dismissed spending time creating outlines. Now I am addicted to the process.

I can't make you cluster and outline, but allow me to say this: If you think the process sounds like a waste of valuable time you could otherwise spend writing, do yourself a small favour and reread the benefits of outlining, especially points *a* to *b*. There *are* reasons for creating outlines.

In addition to the benefits of outlining, you should know that you subconsciously brainstorm and produce an outline as you write.

You are thinking about all that you have to write about as you write and you are thinking about what comes *next* — your next point or two — as you write. This is not a very effective or efficient process.

Clustering and outlining removes the blank page. It replaces it with every point you want to address as you write. It frees the brain to focus on writing from point to point rather than holding on to everything you want to write as you are writing.

Brainstorming first, using clustering, and then producing an outline based on your clustering, will make you a more effective *and* efficient writer.

In other words, by following the process, you will become a better writer and you will actually spend less time overall on your writing. I am not saying it will be easy. I am saying the process detailed here will, however, make the writing easier.

Does Clustering Work?

Let's find out. Before we do, however, allow me to relate what a senior partner of an accounting firm said shortly after I introduced him to clustering.

He had chosen to use a key word associated with a major report he had to write.

After he finished the clustering exercise, he said:

"You freed one gigabyte of RAM. I was holding it all in and you had me pull this outline out of nowhere. Everything I need to know about my report is down on paper. Now that I know what I'm going to say, I have brainpower left to think about how I'm going to say it. It's all over but the writing, and the writing is no longer intimidating."

Clustering Exercise 3

I want you to do one final clustering exercise today. Think of a key word or phrase you associate with any topic you might want to write about. Feel free to cluster a key word or phrase you associate with your book. Ideally, you want to pick a subject about which you have already conducted some research or about which you have extensive knowledge.

The key word or phrase should summarize your topic. Once you have the key word or phrase in mind, write it down and start clustering.

When you are ready, begin clustering using:

What Next?

Now that you have completed your clustering, what next? Now you go mining for gold.

Take a highlighter and highlight words or phrases in your cluster strings that you might consider to be major topics. If you see minor topic points or sub-points, feel free to highlight them too. You might even want to use different highlighter colours for different major and related minor topic points.

If you didn't produce any, or many, topic points, try clustering again. Really focus on the topic you want to write about. If it helps free your mind, use a larger sheet of paper — even flipchart paper. Get down on paper all you associate with your book topic.

Once you are done clustering and highlighting, take a break.

Just so you know, we'll work again with clustering and outlines in a few days; we will apply extensive clustering and outlining exercises directly to your book before you start to write. This is all part of your 60 days.

However, before we come back to clustering and outlining, I want you to look at the formal *writing process*. We will spend some time thinking about and applying various components of the writing process to your book.

Why do we have to spend some time thinking, when we could be writing?

Just as you would not run a mile or a marathon without getting in shape first, you should not write a report or a book without getting in shape first. All of this pre-writing work we are about to do is meant to get you in shape for the writing marathon that you will soon run. So let's stretch and limber up.

Chapter 5: The Writing Process: Day 4

The writing process we are going to use to create your book includes five steps:

1. Preparation
2. Research
3. Organization
4. Writing
5. Revision

Notice that writing is only one of the steps in the writing process.

In the first step, you prepare to write. In the second step, you conduct your research — internal and perhaps external, depending on the scope of the project, your readers' expectations and your knowledge or mastery of the topic. In the third step, you get organized and outline each chapter of your book. Finally, you write. And then you revise.

Get Organized Before You Write

It is critical that you get organized before you write. And while you are writing, you do not revise, edit or proofread. Revision is the final step.

The time required for each step varies with different writing projects and your level of knowledge about the topic. For instance, if you know nothing about rocket science and you decide to write a non-fiction book on rocket science, you will have to do a great deal of external research. If you know a lot about the subject you want to write about, you may not have to do any external research; however, you will still have to pull the information out of your brain and get it down on paper (internal research).

When writing a short e-mail message, you can prepare, research and organize by listing the points you want to cover, while thinking about your audience and purpose. Once you list your points in order, writing should be as simple as turning points into sentences. Then you revise to ensure you have effectively made your primary point(s), thereby achieving your purpose, and you proofread to check spelling and grammar. Then you click "Send".

On the other hand, when writing a formal report or a book, you will spend much more time preparing, researching and organizing. For instance, before writing a book, you should produce a formal outline — an integral component of being organized — and review it in detail. As you write section by section, you might discover gaps in your knowledge. If so, you will have to conduct more research and incorporate the new material into your outline, which serves as a bookmark by holding your place until you come back with the information.

When you finish writing your first draft, you spend time revising to ensure your writing is as clear, concise and as focused as possible. Then you proofread it or have it proofread to correct spelling and grammatical errors.

If you follow this process, you will become a more effective and efficient writer, as studies have demonstrated. According to one study conducted by two professors at the University of Toronto named McLuhan and Davies:

- *Efficient writers spend 40 per cent of their time planning (preparation, research and organization), 25 per cent of their time writing and 35 per cent of their time revising.*
- *Less efficient writers spend more time overall on projects and distribute their time differently: 20 per cent planning, 60 per cent writing (tinkering, writing, tinkering...), and 20 per cent revising, tinkering, revising. In addition to spending more time overall on projects, less efficient writers tend to be less satisfied with the results.*

It may seem ironic to say you can become more efficient if you spend less time writing. However, the time you invest up front — preparing, researching and organizing — pays dividends when it comes time to write and revise.

Think of writing as a journey. If you plan your journey, you are less likely to get lost and more likely to arrive on time. This does not mean you cannot meander as you travel. However, if you meander and your side trip takes you nowhere, you will find it easier to get back on track because you have a road map or, in the case of writing, a process that includes a detailed outline.

Writing Process: Five Step Overview

With that in mind, let's briefly review each component of the five steps in our writing process. We will apply the most significant aspects of the process as we work our way through this book.

1. Preparation
   a. Establish your primary purpose.
   b. Assess your audience and the environment within which they exist and will read your words.

    c. Determine the scope of your coverage or the extent of the detail required to achieve your primary purpose and the primary purpose of your readers.

    d. Select the appropriate medium for delivering your words.

2. Research

    a. Determine if the research will be internal, external or a combination of both.

    b. Find appropriate sources of information and knowledge.

    c. Take notes and document sources.

3. Organization

    a. Select an appropriate method of development so your writing unfolds in a logical manner.

    b. Prepare an outline, breaking your document into manageable sections or chunks.

    c. Consider layout, design and required visuals (photos, illustrations, graphs, charts).

4. Writing

    a. Write from your outline, expanding your points into sentences and paragraphs.

    b. Write with spell check and grammar check turned off so that your internal editor does not distract you as you write.

    c. Complete a first draft of your document, a full section of long documents or a chapter of your book before revising.

5. Revision

    a. Revise with the reader in mind.

    b. Revise to ensure your document is clear, concise, focused and supports your purpose.

    c. Ensure the tone is appropriate for your audience and the subject matter.

    d. Check your spelling and grammar.

    e. Have someone edit and proofread your work.

Again, we will apply the most significant aspects of the process to producing your book. Tomorrow, we start with preparation. Mind you, I have not given you any exercises to do today, so if you are still feeling eager and energetic, read on.

Chapter 6: Preparation: Days 5 & 6

Before you read on, a suggestion: start each day you work on your book with five minutes of freefall. Once you complete your freefall, find a line in it that intrigues you and use it as the opening line for a directed freefall. Or simply use a line that may be on your mind or from a book, newspaper or website and start a five-minute directed freefall.

Think of this as loosening up for the writing marathon you are about to embark on. Few people would start a marathon, or any race for that matter, without stretching first. Freefall and directed freefall are like stretching your mind, getting you ready to write.

As far as this chapter is concerned, you might complete it in a day; however, I am giving you two days to work on it. I don't want you to simply read through it. I want you to read, think and jot down answers to questions, which could take a couple of working days to do.

Getting prepared is what most writers do before they write. You may do this in a subconscious manner but I suggest you do it consciously — by reviewing the preparation points below and writing down your thoughts so they are no longer swirling around in the vortex of your mind with all the other stuff you have to think about. Writing down your thoughts about and ideas for your book makes them real. It is also a way of committing to them.

Before we begin getting prepared, let's review this part of the

writing process.
1. Preparation
    a. Establish your primary purpose.
    b. Assess your audience and the environment within which they exist and will read your words.
    c. Determine the scope of your coverage or the extent of the detail required to achieve your primary purpose and the primary purpose of your readers.
    d. Select the appropriate medium for delivering your words.

Establish Your Primary Purpose

To establish your purpose, answer this question: Why? Why do you want to write what you want to write?

It is conceivable that an honest answer could be, "To make money." Perhaps you give speeches or conduct workshops and want to earn more money by selling your books to those who attend your speeches or workshops. Beyond that, there is a deeper answer to "Why?" — the true purpose of your book.

For instance, I have written several books on the business of freelance writing, writing for newspapers and magazines and writing for corporate markets. You can check them out at www.paullima.com/books. My why goes something like this:

"I am writing my book to educate freelance writers and aspiring freelance writers about the business side of freelance writing."

Now this question begs additional why questions: Why is this important? To whom is it important?

My answer to those questions goes something like this:

"Freelance writers tend not to be business-minded. But freelance writing is a business. Unless freelance writers learn how to conduct themselves in a business-like manner, they might be exploited or they simply might fail at their business."

As you can see, my purpose, or why, is clear. So is my audience. I want to educate freelance writers. And, as you can see, there is a reason for my purpose: "Unless freelance writers learn how to conduct themselves in a business-like manner, they might be exploited or they simply might fail at their business." In other words, I believe my purpose fills a need. And if I am right, if the need exists, then there is a market for my books.

The answers to *why* help me focus on a particular audience, known as a target market, and help me focus the content of my books on the needs of my target market. In short, my books focus on the business of freelance writing and are written primarily for new and aspiring freelance writers.

For a book to be a success, focus is critical. The book has to focus on something for someone. You find your focus when you find your audience, your purpose and your rationale for your purpose.

What if you want to write your family history? Why would you want to do that? To tell your family story, no doubt. However, I presume there is something of particular interest about your family story that helps you answer a bigger why question. Perhaps your family overcame adversity or tragedy. Perhaps your family went from rags to riches or riches to rags. In other words, are there life lessons to be learned from reading your family story? If so, who would be most interested in learning them?

Whether you are writing about business, health, science, motivation or telling a personal story, find and write down your purpose and your rationale for it. Write it down to keep yourself focused. If you ever find yourself meandering, go back to your purpose and refocus your effort.

Before you move on, answer your whys in writing. Answer the questions below. Feel free to revise the questions to suit your particular book, and then answer them. But don't move on until you answer them:

- Why do you want to write what you want to write?
- What is the true purpose of your book?
- Why is your book important?
- Who will find your book important?
- Why will your target market find your book important?

Before you move on, I want you to answer one final question. To answer this question, you have to imagine yourself as a prospective buyer of your book. In other words, try to look at your book idea from the point of view of your target market. With that perspective in mind, answer this:

- What's in it for me?

There must be something in your book that will be of benefit to the reader. You need to know what it is. Knowing what's in it for your reader will help keep your writing focused. In addition, it will help you write any marketing material you use to promote your book. I know we are getting ahead of ourselves by thinking about marketing material now — we still have to write the book — but your marketing material is based on your most pertinent book content. And the most pertinent content of your book is what will make prospective readers pause and say, "Ah, that's what's in it for me!"

So anchor your thoughts. Answer the above questions, in writing, not just in your mind, before you move on.

Assess Your Audience

I want to take a moment here to focus on your audience, although we have started to do so with the answers to our why questions.

Before you begin to write, try to visualize your audience. Get a solid image in your mind. After all, these are the people for whom you will be writing. Answer the questions below. Don't just ruminate on them. Again, write down your answers. Doing so makes your thoughts real and enables you to write more effectively, with greater focus and clarity.

Thinking about your potential audience, ask yourself:

What is the Language Skill Level of my Audience?

If you are writing for an audience with a variety of language skill levels, ascertain the language skill of the primary readers — those most likely to buy your book. If the language skills vary, keep your document as simple as possible or use glossaries and definitions to explain complex concepts and terminology.

What is the Technical Skill Level of my Audience?

If you are writing a technical document for an audience with a wide range of technical skills or understanding, determine the technical knowledge of the primary readers. If the readers' technical knowledge varies, keep your document as simple as possible. If appropriate to the content, include required technical details in appendices at the end of the book. Use glossaries and definitions to explain complex concepts and terminology.

What Are My Readers' Expectations?

Are your readers expecting to be entertained or informed? Educated or sold? Coddled or persuaded? Should you meet those expectations or defy them for effect? Can you, should you, manipulate their expectations? Answers to these questions will help you determine the tone of your writing and resolve content issues.

In What Context will the Document be Received?

For example, are you writing for a sceptical audience, one with a number of built-in objections? Or are you writing for the faithful, those who support your purpose and want their support reinforced? Answers to these questions will also help you determine the tone of your writing and resolve content issues.

What is the Greatest Need or Desire of My Audience?

Are you writing for those who want to learn more about a topic for the pleasure of learning or those who want to learn more so they can take a particular action? Are you writing for those who want to avoid taking action, or who want to minimize the cost or energy associated with taking a particular action? Are you writing for those who want to be better informed about an issue or those who simply want to be entertained?

A need is different from a desire.

The reader might need to find food, shelter or security, which might involve learning a new skill such as how to hunt, grow food or cook, how to build a shelter, how to defend one's self or how to earn money. The reader might need to improve his or her health, which might involve learning about nutrition, exercise, alternative medicine and so on.

The reader might desire or wish to boost his or her income, become more attractive, dance better, use a computer more effectively, attract the opposite sex (or same sex), travel on a budget, and so on. This too might involve making more money, learning new skills or techniques.

As the writer, you have to know if you are fulfilling a need, a desire or a bit of both. And you must determine the kind of information you have to convey to satisfy the need or fulfil the desire. Thinking about the big picture, jot down the needs or desires you want to meet or fulfill. Again, doing this will help get you focused before you begin to write.

In short, if you are not writing with a pre-defined purpose for a pre-defined audience with a pre-defined need or desire, you are most likely writing for nobody. Because, try as you might, you cannot be all things to all people.

Your Reader's Environment

It is also important that you know the context or the environment within which your primary readers exist and will read your book.

For instance, for my freelance writing books, I see my audience as being writers or aspiring writers. That means they most likely have some university or college education. I see them reading the book at home. It could be they have a full-time job and want to leave it to start freelancing. They are reasonably intelligent people who may lack the courage to make the leap into freelance writing.

However, they may also be working as freelancers and may be feeling frustrated by the lack of money they are earning or the type of work they are doing. They may be thinking they should leave the business and get a real job, but would rather stay, boost their business and become successful.

Knowing this helps me ask some important questions:

- What does my audience want to achieve?
- What does my audience need to know to achieve it?
- How much detail do they require to achieve their objectives?
- In what order do should I convey the information?

Notice that I am concerned about the readers' objectives, not my objectives.

Knowing who my readers are and knowing what they need helps me establish the tone of my writing and it influences content. For my books, the tone should be educational or how-to. The content should spell out in detail the steps readers need to go through, and the order in which they need to go through them, if they want to achieve success as freelance writers.

Can you see how this will influence the concepts I will address, the order in which I will address them and the detail I will use to address them? In short, this knowledge will literally influence the words I use when writing my book. Best to know it now, before I start writing.

Let's briefly look at another example.

I have a different audience in mind for my *Copywriting that Works* book. Many freelance writers and individuals who work in advertising and marketing buy my copywriting book. My primary readers, though, are students who want to learn about copywriting or junior copywriters who want to advance their careers, which they often do by taking copywriting courses.

Although students will be using the book, my primary target market is the college or university copywriting instructor who approves the book for use in a copywriting course. Teachers have to feel my book will help their students, so I've included many exercises and case studies, which are of benefit to any reader. Of course, instructors can turn the exercises into assignments, saving them course preparation time.

It stands to reason that if my primary reader is the copywriting student and my primary target market is the copywriting instructor, a copywriting book that is of benefit to both students and instructors will be better than one that is only of benefit to students or instructors. Ironically, a copywriting book that is of benefit to both students and instructors makes for a better book overall.

So spend some time and assess your audience. After all, that is who you will be writing for.

Determine Your Scope

Before writing your book, it is important that you determine the scope of your coverage. What degree of detail do you need to achieve your purpose? What degree of detail do you need to help your readers achieve their purpose? In short, what do your readers need to know or learn so they can do what you want to help them do and what they want to do?

Again, thinking big picture, make sure you have answered, in writing, the following questions:

- What is my primary purpose?
- Who are my primary readers?
- What does my audience already know?
- What does my audience need to know?
- In what order should I convey the points they need to know?

- How much detail do they require to achieve their objectives?

When answering the questions, you do not have to list every point you are going to cover in your book. Try to jot down the major topic points, and then take a bit of time and organize them in a logical order.

Feel free to use point form or whatever helps you get the information out of your mind and down on paper. In other words, start to make what you are going to write real; don't hold onto it in your head.

We are going to do more work on this; however, spend a bit of time now and create a skeletal outline based on what your reader knows and needs to know in order to accomplish the purpose of the book.

At the risk of being redundant, allow me to repeat: Having answers to these questions in advance will bring focus to your writing. Knowing the answers will make you a more effective writer.

Select an Appropriate Medium

Although you've already likely decided your medium will be a book, it doesn't hurt to ask yourself if it should be a hardcover book, paperback or PDF file, if it should be an audio CD or if you should use some other medium to convey your words. Also, if you want to publish a book — and books are still a popular and effective medium — think about the physical aspects.

For instance, if you are producing a workbook, you might want it to be 8½ by 11 inches and spiral bound so that it readers can easily work from it. A 6 by 9 trade paperback, like this book, is easy to read anywhere or carry around. How do you see your book being used? What size and binding is appropriate for your book?

Don't be concerned if you can't answer these questions now. You often answer them in conjunction with your agent or publisher. But it is worth thinking about them, especially if you are planning to self-publish. If that is the case, do some research. Look at other books in your field. Get some feedback from a few people you think may be potential readers. Also, talk to printers or print-on-demand companies. You might find out that the book size or type of binding you had in mind might make your book cost-prohibitive.

Again, don't spend too much time on this here. Get the book written first. But keep this in mind.

Finally, when thinking about your book, ask yourself if you need charts, graphics, illustrations or photos. If so (again, you don't have to decide now), will you create them or find third-party sources to supply them? If you are thinking of running full-colour images and photos, you have to know that doing so can make your book cost-prohibitive. So look at a lot of books and, over time, make some decisions concerning your medium.

While we haven't started to write yet, I hope you can see how spending time planning is going to make it easier for you to write and how it is going to make your writing more focused and effective, keeping you on topic and helping you convey information your readers need to know.

Before you create a formal outline and start to write, I want you to take a day to consider your research process.

Chapter 7: Research: Day 7

I want to remind you to start each day with five minutes of freefall followed by five minutes of directed freefall. The time you invest in stretching and exercising now will help you avoid writer's cramp later, when you are actually writing your book.

Of course, if anything you can use in your book comes up while you freefall, as it often does, consider it a bonus.

Internal and External Research

Extensive external research is not part of the 60-day book writing process. As I said previously, if you want to write about rocket science and you know nothing about rocket science, you have a lot of external research to do — more than 60 days worth, I would imagine.

If you want to write a family history that starts with the first generation on your family tree and you have not traced your family's genealogy, you have a lot of work to do before you can outline your book and start writing.

However, I suspect you are most likely an expert in your field. If this is the case, most of the research you have to do is internal — you have to pull what you know about your topic out of your cranium and put it down on paper.

You will actually conduct your internal research as you move through the next sections of this book. You will use the results of your internal research — pulling information out of your brain and getting it down on paper — to create your outline.

That being said, only you can determine if the research you need to do will be external, internal or a combination of both. So I want you to spend some time thinking about what you know and what you need to know before you can write your book.

Document Your Research

If you have to conduct external research, it is up to you to find appropriate sources of information, take notes and document your sources. Again, how to do so goes beyond the scope of this book. However, when conducting external research, be as thorough as you can be and document all of your sources because you may have to reference them in your book.

When documenting sources, include details such as:

- Names and titles of people you interview.
- Companies or organizations they work for or organizations they are associated with.
- Dates and locations of interviews.
- Authors, publishers and dates of publication of all books you read and may want to cite in your book.
- Addresses of all websites you visit.
- Any other facts you can think of that would be pertinent to documenting your sources.

You will need to use this information to document any claims you make in your book. Documenting claims — especially if you are not an expert in the field, or if you want to cite other experts in the field — gives you greater credibility. Also, attributing any sources you cite is just good form.

In short, either you have the information you want to write about or you will conduct external research to acquire the information you want to write about.

Whether you use external research sources or have a great deal of knowledge, at some point you have to move information from your head to the page. The question is: How do you do this?

Cluster. Outline. Write.

Clustering helps you get down on paper all that you know about your subject. Outlining helps you organize your material in a logical manner. And writing lets you convert your outline into coherent sentences and well structured paragraphs.

Before you cluster, outline and write, as you will soon be doing, ask yourself if you have to do any additional research. If so, take time to acquire the knowledge you need to write your book. Keep track of your research sources. If you do not have to do any additional external research, it's time to get organized.

Again, there were no exercises to do today. Feel free to take the rest of the day off. However, if you are feeling energetic, read on.

Chapter 8: Get Organized I: Day 8

A part of me wants to call this section *From Clustering to Outline to First Draft — Day 8 to 60*. The reason for this is simple. Here is what you will do with the rest of your time:

- Extensively cluster key words or phrases related to your book.
- Create a detailed, chapter by chapter outline.
- Write from outline point to outline point until you finish your first draft.

After writing, you edit and proofread or find someone to do it for you. Then you look for an agent or publisher or you self-publish your book. The End.

In fact, if you understand the process I've described, you may be chomping at the bit to start. However, I suspect you'd feel a tad disappointed, and perhaps a bit confused, if I said go to it and ended the book here.

Remember what I said about your book having to meet your readers' expectations if you want it to be a success?

It's fair to say that you expect me to tell you in detail exactly how to apply clustering and outlining to your book, and I am going to guide you through the process. I will give you explicit instructions as to what you do; it will be up to you to work diligently at it and do it.

Create a Logical Flow

To start with, let's look at what we mean by organization. The first thing you need to do is select an appropriate method of development so your writing unfolds in a logical manner.

Let's say you were writing instructions for a software application. You would present information in the order the reader should do things. For instance, after an introduction explaining the function of the application — something you would reinforce even though the reader, having bought the software, should know what it does — you might start with how to open the application. Why "might"? Perhaps you need to tell the reader how to install the application on his or her computer first. Only you, as the subject expert, can make this decision. It also depends on who your readers are, what they expect and what you have promised them in your promotional material.

Once you help the reader install and open the application, you reveal what to do next: perhaps enter basic information and save the file. Then you escalate the complexity, starting with the most common functions readers generally perform and moving to functions that are more esoteric. Of course, if your book was "for beginners" you might not move far beyond the basic functions. If you are writing an advanced book, you might present an overview of the basic functions and quickly get to the more esoteric ones — again, building in a logical manner.

If you are presenting a family history, you could start at the very beginning of the family. However, writing that unfolds in a logical manner does not necessarily have to unfold in chronological order. For instance, you might want to start in the present, illustrate the state of the family today, and then take your readers back to the beginning so they can see how the family got from where it was to where it is.

Logic Depends On...

The logic depends on your subject, your purpose and your reader — what the reader already knows and what the reader needs to know, and the order in which the reader needs to know it to achieve the desired purpose of the book.

There is a logical flow to the development of my *Copywriting That Works* book (www.paullima.com/books). I start with an introduction to the book, of course, followed by an overview of how the advertising industry works and the role of the copywriter within the industry. Before I get the reader to start writing, I look at creativity in advertising. I am, after all, going to ask readers to be creative so I want them to understand how to apply various creative techniques to copywriting. I also give the readers an overview of the writing process, as I have done here. Then I look at the need to know your target market and ad purpose, how to write headlines and copy blocks and so on. When it comes to writing, I move from a discussion on writing one-page ads to writing more complex direct response marketing brochures.

The logic is based on what readers need to know first, before they learn what they need to know next. Granted, some readers might already know the first couple of steps. However, as an author, you cannot presume this. Or, if you are going to presume it, then you have to let the reader know what you expect them to know before they plunge into your book. You try to do this in your title. For example, a book entitled, *Excel for Advanced Power Users* is obviously not a book for Excel beginners. You also convey this information in any promotional copy used to promote your book and on the cover and back cover of your book.

What I want you to do now is select an appropriate method of development so your writing unfolds in a logical manner.

Revisit Purpose

Before you start to think about what the reader knows, or needs to know, before reading your book, I want you to think about your topic and the purpose of your book again. If you don't have this information written down, write it down now on a sheet of paper or in a word processing file.

Simply finish these two statements:

- The topic of my book is…
- The purpose of my book is…

Having this information in front of you will help keep you focused as you think about what the reader knows and the information you have to convey.

Once you have written down the information, read on.

What the Reader Knows

Under the title What the Reader Knows, jot down in point form everything that readers most likely know, or should know, before reading your book.

What you are doing here is setting a common knowledge denominator — what your reader knows, or should know, before reading your book. You will most likely not address these topics in your book, or you will not address them in detail beyond overview remarks in an introductory chapter.

This common knowledge denominator will help you determine the scope of your book and will help you write promotional copy targeted at the person who would most likely benefit from, and therefore buy, your book. In other words, not everyone should read your book. Some people need to acquire knowledge that would enable them to understand what you are writing about; others already possess the information you are conveying in your book.

Allow me to expand on this point.

If your book is about bookkeeping, I need to have basic math skills to apply the information you are presenting. If your book is about Computer Aided Design (CAD), I should have basic design skills, which you might teach me in another book.

This book is about how to write a non-fiction book. If you have no idea what you want to write about, you will be hard pressed to complete any of the exercises included here. So think about what your reader knows or needs to know, before reading your book.

Write down this information now, under the title *What the reader knows* — point form is fine — and then read on.

What the Reader Will Know

Using broad strokes, I now want you to jot down what you want the reader to learn or what the reader will know when he or she finishes your book. Start with *What the Reader will Know* as your title and jot down the points the reader will *learn*. Again, using point form here is fine.

I used learn in italics because your book may not teach and, in fact, the reader may not be reading to learn, although most non-fiction books teach and non-fiction readers often want to learn.

Even if learning, in the traditional sense of the word, is not what your book is about, learning is often a subset of purpose. For instance, your purpose might be to have readers take a particular action. But they still need to acquire information or learn something about a cause or issue before they can act. You might want to inform your readers about issues so they can make more informed decisions. The reader must still acquire information in a logical manner before doing so. This is a lot like learning.

On the other hand, you may want to entertain readers. Your tale must still unfold in a logical manner or the reader will be confused. There is something you must reveal first, before the reader can absorb the next point, and so on. This, too, is like learning.

Again, what I want you to do here is jot down the major points the reader must absorb, process or learn to fulfill the purpose of your book and to meet their expectations.

How many points should you jot down? There is nothing wrong with getting detailed, but feel free to use broad strokes here — think major topic points. It could be 15 or 20 major topic points. It may be more; it may be less. You will refine this list as you move forward and get organized, so don't sweat the number of points. Simply jot down as many points as possible. As you are producing this list of major topic points, you may also produce a number of sub-points. Feel free to jot down any sub-points under the appropriate major topic points. However, don't pressure yourself to jot down every minor detail that will go into your book.

So go ahead, under the title *What the Reader will Know*, make a list of major topic points your readers will learn about when they read your book.

Organize Your List

Once you have created your list of what your reader will learn, I want you to review it and think about how to order the points to facilitate the learning process. In other words, arrange the topic points and any related sub-points in the order in which you think you should present them.

Once you have ordered your topic points, put away the list.

What you have completed here is a linear or left-brain exercise. In the next chapter, I am going to have you do something similar. However, I am going to have you take a right-brain approach to it.

How do we use the right side of our brain to do what we have just done with the left side? Read on.

If you want to make this right-brain process work for you, do not read on though until you have completed the exercises described above.

Just so you know, once you have completed the right-brain work, you are going to create the most comprehensive list, or book outline, possible.

Then you write.

So stop chomping at the bit. You are getting close to writing your book!

Get Organized II: Day 9

One last reminder: Start each day you work on your book with five minutes of freefall followed by five minutes of directed freefall. When you get to writing the book, you can stop freefalling — if you are so inclined. However, freefall is a great way to clear the mind before you write, kind of like stretching before a race. I recommend that you freefall daily; you can decide if doing so is useful.

Clustering Revisited

You have done a fair bit of preparation, thinking and left-brain work related to your book. Your mind is now more focused on what you want to write, why you want to write it and for whom you want to write it. You even have a decent sense of the various topics you need to write about.

Therefore, I don't want you to pull your previous clustering work out of a drawer. We have moved beyond that initial work. Instead, I want you to do some new clustering work. If you need to, review the clustering section of this book before you begin. Otherwise, carry on. The work you do here will help you prepare both a solid big picture outline and a more detailed, chapter by chapter outline of your book.

Here is what I want you to do:

- Get several sheets of blank paper and a pen that works.

Literally, have 20 or more sheets handy. You can use 8½ by 11 sheets of paper, but you might want to use larger sheets — even flipchart paper.

- Pick a key word or phrase that represents the subject or topic of your book. Think on this and pick something pithy that focuses in on your subject matter.

  For my *Copywriting that Works* book, I used *copywriting*. For my *Business of Freelance Writing* (for newspapers and magazines) book, I used *Freelance Writing — Periodicals*. For *The Six-Figure Freelancer* (freelancing for corporate markets), I used *Freelancing — Corporate*. For my *Search Engine Optimization* book, I simply used *SEO*. For my *How to Write Media Releases* book, I used *Media Releases*.

- Write down your key word or phrase.

- Underline it.

- Circle it.

- Cluster it. *But*, before you do your clustering, please read on.

The Idea Mother Lode

You might be wondering why I asked you to have lots of paper handy. Sometimes, as you cluster, you will hit what I call an idea mother lode — a cluster vein that is so rich that you want to use the first word or phrase in the vein as a new key word on a separate sheet of paper. If you find such a word — often it represents a section or chapter title — move to a clean sheet of paper and cluster it.

On the other hand, you could be several words or phrases into a cluster string before you realize you've found a goldmine. That's all right. Grab a clean sheet of paper and start to cluster the first word or phrase in the rich cluster string. For instance, when I clustered

Freelance Writing — *Periodicals*, I hit a number of veins that deserved their own clusters. Veins included Job Description, Article Ideas, Portfolio, Query Letter, Article Lead, Interview and many others.

I suspect you have a sense of what we are doing here. We are getting down on paper, using the right-brain technique of clustering, all we know about and associate with our subject matter. We are creating mental space so we no longer have to hold onto it all. The reason we are using a number of sheets of paper is simple. One sheet is not big enough to hold all we know about a topic — not if we know enough to write a book about it. Each new sheet we start represents a significant book topic, section or chapter.

At the same time, it is possible that through your left-brain work in Chapter 8 you have down on paper several dozen points, each representing a significant book topic, chapter or section. You might think you have down on paper all the topic points you need to cover in your book. I still want you to cluster a "big picture word" that represents your book. You could surprise yourself and discover missing topics, sections or chapters. Once you have completed your clustering, add any new topics, sections or chapters to your *What the Reader will Know* list you created in Chapter 8. Once you have that list complete, you cluster each point on it.

However, don't start your clustering yet. I will soon explain in more detail the two approaches you can take to this exercise. No matter how you approach this exercise, key to it all is that you create as comprehensive a list as possible of topics, sections and chapters you will address in your book, and that you cluster in detail each topic, section or chapter that you have created.

Just so you know, you are going to devote the rest of this chapter to a comprehensive clustering of your subject matter and all the topics related to it. It may not feel like it yet, but you are so very close to the state any writer wants to achieve — the state where *it's all over but the writing*.

So go. Pick a key word or phrase that represents the subject of your book. As you have seen from my example, the word or phrase does not have to be anything fancy or convoluted. It should be something pithy and representative of your book's subject matter or purpose.

Get a fresh sheet of paper, jot down that word or phrase. Underline it. Circle it. And cluster it. At least do that in a moment. Read on a bit more first.

How Much Time Should I Spend on This?

If you only spend 10 or 15 minutes on this, you have not worked diligently at it. If you spend 30 minutes or so, you still have not spent enough time at it. This process can easily take you several hours. Having said that, it is not the time that counts. It is the results that count.

By the time you finish this process, you should have pages and pages and pages of clusters, all related to your subject matter. Each page represents a major topic point and contains numerous sub-points related to the major topic. This is internal research at its finest.

By the end of this process, you will have produced numerous excellent nuggets — material and information you *must* include in your book. Some of your pages will be more detailed than others, which is to be expected. If you are clustering as freely as possible, some of your cluster strings might seem as if they are off-topic. Not a problem. It happens. Go with the flow. Sometimes you have to go off-topic to get back on-topic.

You can say that you would have produced or found the information anyway. I won't argue with you. But I will ask you this: When and how would you have found the information? In other words, since you have to go looking for it in order to find it, use clustering to help you find it here and now. Get it out of your mind and down on paper so you can let go of it but not lose it.

Get Ready to Cluster

As mentioned, you are going to be here a while. If need be, get a drink, go to the washroom or take a good stretch now, before you begin.

There are two ways you can approach this exercise. They both start the same way, as follows:

- Get a fresh sheet of paper.
- Jot down your key word or phrase.
- Underline it and circle it.
- Cluster it.

One Way

As your clustering generates a new major topic, move to a clean sheet of paper and cluster your new topic on the new sheet of paper. Once you are done, resume your "big picture" clustering. As you generate a new major topic, move to a clean sheet of paper and repeat the process.

Once you are done, review the list you created in Chapter 8. If some of the items on the list did not come up in today's work, treat them like major topics to be clustered. Jot down a key word or phrase representing such topics and cluster them too.

By time you are finished, you should have a cluster sheet for each of the major topics that you will address in your book. On each sheet, you should have a series of sub-points related to your major point.

The Other Way

On the other hand, if you like to take a more linear approach to right-brain exercises, cluster your key word or phrase extensively, generating as many "big picture" topics as you can. Don't sweat the minor points; don't ignore them if they come up, but focus on producing an inner circle of major points related to your key word or phrase.

Cluster as extensively as possible and then compare your cluster to the list you created in the last chapter. Add any new points to your list.

Once you have a comprehensive list, cluster each of the points on a clean sheet of paper to generate sub-points for every major topic point.

By time you are finished, you should have a cluster sheet for each of the major topics that you will address in your book. On each sheet, you should have a series of sub-points related to your major point.

- Pick the method you want to use for the exercise. Pick your key word or phrase. Write it down. Underline it. Circle it. Start to cluster.

- Continue this process until you have exhausted your clustering, until you have down on paper all you know about and associate with the subject of your book and each major topic you want to cover in your book.

[Please complete this process before you read on.]

Go. Do it.

This is an important and crucial stage in the development of your book. This is getting everything down on paper you associate with your subject. This is you on your way to the point at which *it is all over but the writing*. We still have one more stage to go before we get to that point, but if you do all of the above, you will be so close.

And you are only *nine* days into this project.

Chapter 10: Get Organized III: Day 10

On Day 10, we take a deep breath and relax before we learn what we are going to do for the next 20 days. Each day takes us closer and closer to that magical place where it is all over but the writing. Then of course, we have 30 days to write.

If you cannot yet imagine writing the first draft of your book in 30 days, stay with me. You will be able to imagine it after you complete your chapter by chapter outline, which we are going to start here.

The Outline

Each day, for the next 20 days, you are going to prepare an outline. You are going to break your book into manageable chunks or chapters and you are going to chunk each chapter into sections. Many of your sections will be further subdivided. The more detailed your outline, the easier it will be to write your book.

If your book only has 10 chapters, you might actually complete this task in 10 days. If your book has 25 or 30 chapters, it might take you longer to do this.

All this, however, begs the question: How long should a chapter be? There is no definitive answer other than "a chapter should be long enough to cover its topic in appropriate detail."

In my books, chapters range in length from a couple of pages to 15 or more pages. What is important is each chapter introduces a topic related to the main subject of the book and gives readers enough information so they can learn what they need to learn, or do what they need to do, before moving on to the next chapter.

Our mantra, as you may recall, is this: Select an appropriate method of development so your writing unfolds in a logical manner. The order of chapters and the degree of information presented in each one facilitate this process.

How to Create the Outline

That being said, we still need to prepare our chapter outlines. Let's say we were writing a book entitled Creating Book Outlines. We'd open a word processing file and jot down our book title, like so:

- Creating Book Outlines.

Below our title, we'd jot down Chapter 1 and the title of the chapter or a working title that lets us know what chapter one is all about, like so:

Chapter 1: How to Create an Outline.

Below our chapter title, we'd jot down the major points we want to cover in the chapter. In our How to Create an Outline chapter, we would cover the following points:

1. Outline major topic points.
2. Subdivide topic headings where appropriate.
3. Further subdivide sub-categories if appropriate.

Let's say Chapter 2 of our book covered Benefits of Outlining. This is what our outline might look like:

Chapter 2: Benefits of Outlining
1. Provides logical structure.
2. Gives you a detailed road map.
3. Ensures all major and minor points are covered.
4. Produces greater clarity and focus.
5. Removes the stress of trying to hold onto all you know about a topic while you are writing about it.
6. Helps you detect errors in logic.
7. Allows you to write quickly in manageable chunks.
8. Ensures you do not lose your train of thought when you have to take breaks from writing.
9. Facilitates the approval process, if one is required.

As you can see, we have nine points to cover in the chapter on Benefits of Outlining. They are fairly large points. However, our outline is not yet complete. Notice the last two points in Chapter 1 of Creating Outlines:

• Subdivide topic headings where appropriate.
• Further subdivide sub-categories if appropriate.

The subject of our book is creating outlines. So far, we have subdivided it into two chapters: "How to Create an Outline" and "Benefits of Outlining." We have further subdivided each of these chapters.

Our goal is to produce as detailed an outline as possible for each chapter of our book. With that in mind, we subdivide, where appropriate, the topics that make up each chapter. This pre-writing outline work will enable you to write more effectively and efficiently.

In short, each chapter outline would look something like this:
Chapter 1: Major topic of chapter
1. Major point 1

      a. Sub-point 1
      b. Sub-point 2
2. Major point 2
      a. Sub-point 1
      b. Sub-point 2
      c. Sub-point 3
      d. Sub-point 4
3. Major point 3
      a. Sub-point 1
      b. Sub-point 2

It is conceivable that you may even have some secondary and tertiary sub-points, such as:

4. Major point 4
      a. Sub-point 1
            i. Secondary point A
      b. Sub-point 2
            i. Secondary point A
           ii. Secondary point B
      c. Sub-point 3
      d. Sub-point 4
      e. Secondary point A
      f. Secondary point B
            i. Tertiary point i
           ii. Tertiary point ii
      g. Secondary point C

It's All Over but the Writing

How many major points, sub-points and sub-sub-points should you have? As many as it takes to create a detailed outline of the entire chapter. Having a detailed outline gets you to that place where it's all over but the writing. The outline is the magic that makes you a much more effective and efficient writer.

Where do you find all these points for your outline? Return to the work you did on Days 8 and 9.

Day 8: You worked in a linear fashion, using broad strokes, and jotted down many major topic points or chapter points. As you produced your list of major topic points, you may have also produced a number of minor points or sub-points under various major topic points. Finally, you arranged the topic points and any related sub-points in the order in which you thought you should present them. Great start.

Day 9: You clustered extensively using a key word or phrase representing your book's subject matter. As major points came up, you clustered them on separate sheets of paper. You also clustered any additional points that were on your Day 8 list. In short, using this right-brain technique you got down on paper all you know about and associate with the various topics that make up your book.

Putting it All Together

Now it's time to go back into left-brain mode. To do so, you incorporate all your clustering material with all that you produced on Day 8.

Your Day 8 work should give you a skeletal outline. If you produced sub-points, you might even have some flesh on the bones of your outline. Your clustering might have produced some new bones for your skeleton, which you have incorporated into the Day 8 outline. In addition, your clustering should have produced a lot more information, sub-points and sub-sub-points of the major topic points, for you to wrap around the bones of your outline. You have not done that yet, but the information is there in all your cluster sheets.

In other words, what you are going to do next is mesh your Day 9 clustering with your Day 8 list. By doing so, you should be able to produce a detailed outline of your book. I am not saying 100 per cent of your outline material is now in front of you; however, if you worked diligently on Days 8 and 9, most of it is there. It is now your job, over the next 20 days, to produce a detailed outline for each chapter — one outline per day.

Again, if you have more than 20 chapters, it may take you a bit longer. If you have fewer chapters, you will be done sooner. If you have time to produce two or three outlines per day, you will finish this in half the time. In addition, the number of days it takes you could change based on the scope and nature of your project.

For the most part, you should be able to complete one detailed chapter outline per day.

Let me be More Concrete

In theory, you might have 20 chapters, each with 10 to 20 points. Many of the points will be divided into five or more secondary and tertiary points. Each day, I want you to produce one chapter title, reflecting the topic of the chapter, and 10 to 20 (or more) points, each with an appropriate number of secondary and tertiary points.

What do you do once you complete an outline of a chapter based on your Day 8 and Day 9 work? You look at it and ask yourself if anything is missing, if there are any other details you can or should add so your book can progress in a logical manner and fulfil your purpose and your readers' expectations.

One way to find out if anything is missing is to grab a pen and writing pad and walk away from your computer after you have completed a chapter outline that is as detailed as possible. I am not talking about simply walking into another room. I am suggesting you literally take a walk or go to a coffee shop.

Sometimes the way to find missing information is to walk away from your primary workspace. Your brain, reasonably distracted, will often serve up information you didn't know you were looking for. Clustering gets most of it out, but there are often one or two stubborn points hiding somewhere in the clutter of your mind. They only come out if you seem distracted, which is why you take the pen and pad of paper with you. If your brain serves up information and you don't write it down, you could very well forget it by the time you get home. I am speaking from personal experience here!

I am suggesting you take 20 days for this detailed outlining process — one day per chapter. Again, if your book is longer than 20 chapters, you might need more time. If your book is shorter, you might take less time. At minimum, you should outline one chapter per working day. If you have time and energy, you could outline a couple of chapters in a day.

No matter what, your goal remains the same when producing your outline: To be as comprehensive and logical as possible, in terms of the content and flow of each chapter and the overall content and flow of your book.

What you want to do over the next 20 days is to get to the point where you are truly ready to write. A detailed, comprehensive outline gets you to that point.

So that is your job. But allow me to cover a couple other points before you start the next 20 days.

Layout, Design and Visuals

Part of getting organized involves considering layout, design and required visuals (photos, illustrations, graphs, charts). Do not spend too much time on layout and design at this point.

I know some people who become preoccupied with layout and design before they outline or write. Most of them never get around to outlining, let alone writing. They spend all their time picking fonts and designing the look of their pages and such, which might be fine if you are producing a full-colour, fully illustrated coffee table book.

But you still have to write the book, and I am strongly suggesting you do that — write it — first.

Layout and design, cover art and so on is organizational work you do after you have written your book. If you find a publisher, you might not even be involved in these aspects of your book. If you are self-publishing and have limited design skills, you may want to contract out these tasks. So do yourself a favour and don't get hung up on layout and design now.

However, as you are outlining your book, think in terms of *appropriate* images, photos, charts, tables or other graphics. Notice how "appropriate" is in italics. Many books have few, if any images, photos, charts, tables or other graphics.

If you can appropriately illustrate any of the points you want to make in your book, jot something down beside the appropriate outline point. It could be as simple as "illustration of elephant here" or "pie chart of research stats here" or "photo of ad with attention-grabbing image here." This lets you know what you think would be appropriate, in terms of graphics, and where it would be appropriate to use them.

After the book is written, you can create or find images for your book.

Getting Even More Organized

Part of getting organized involves considering appropriate examples, how-to information, definitions and exercises, and indicating where to place them in your outline. It is conceivable that appropriate examples, how-to information, definitions and exercises came up in your Day 8 linear work or, more likely, in your Day 9 clustering. If not, don't worry. After you produce a chapter outline, review it and ask yourself if you require any examples, how-to information, definitions or exercises.

By way of example, my *How to Write Media Releases* book would not be an effective book if it did not include examples of media releases and media advisories. In fact, I include generic templates of both. In addition, I include media release examples that follow the template and a couple that break free from the formal format. However, my examples would not be effective if I did not spell out, in detail, how to construct media releases and advisories. My how-to instructions would be less effective if I had not defined, compared and contrasted releases and advisories.

In addition, I give the readers a few suggested exercises to help motivate them to apply what they learn. That being said, I did not define, describe "how to" and present examples in the same chapter.

As mentioned previously, there is a logical flow to the development of a book. The logic is based on what readers need to know first before they can learn what they need to know next. So you have to logically choose where you will place definitions, how-to instructions, examples and exercises.

It could be they all appear in one chapter, especially if your book requires readers to understand a definition, see an example and learn how to do something, or if it requires them to learn how to do *A* well before they can do *B*.

In my case, it made sense to define media releases and advisories first and then talk about the factors that influence when you use one or the other. Once the readers had definitions, the knowledge of which one to use under what circumstances and had seen examples, they were ready for a step-by-step process concerning how to write releases and advisories.

With that in mind, outline your chapters, determine where you might want to insert graphics and where you might want to insert definitions, how-to information, examples and exercises.

Be as thorough and comprehensive with your outline as possible. The time you spend here will pay off in spades later, when it comes to writing.

Now, on With the Show. Almost.

Do read the next section before you produce your first outline.

Chapter 11: Producing Outlines: Days 11 to 31

In some ways, much of my work here is done. I do not have much more to say other than go do it — go produce those outlines. Although I have shown you examples of outlines, I would like to show you a detailed outline from one of my books. But first, I want to show you what happens to those major topics points — how they become chapter titles and make up the table of contents.

Table of Contents is Just an Outline

Here is the table of contents from *The Business of Freelance Writing: How to Develop Article Ideas and Sell Them to Newspapers and Magazines*:

Chapter 1: About the Book and Author
Chapter 2: What Freelance Writers Do?
Chapter 3: Reality Check & Getting Started
Chapter 4: Know Your Editor and Audience
Chapter 5: Time Management
Chapter 6: Do the Math
Chapter 7: Article Ideas: Clustering
Chapter 8: Article Ideas: Developing Your Own
Chapter 9: Developing More Article Ideas
Chapter 10: Building Your Portfolio

Chapter 11: Querying Editors: Overview
Chapter 12: Sample Query Letters
Chapter 13: More Sample Query Letters
Chapter 14: 21 Rules for Writing Stellar Query Letters
Chapter 15: Multiple Submissions & Follow Up
Chapter 16: Before Writing the Article Lead
Chapter 17: Feature Article Leads
Chapter 18: Finding Markets
Chapter 19: Idea Acceptance: Now What?
Chapter 20: Research and Interviews
Chapter 21: Copyright & Other Business Issues
Chapter 22: Additional Sample Query Letters

With that information in place before I start to write, I know I have to write 22 chapters to produce my book. I also know what each chapter will be about. I can then step back, assess my chapter titles and ascertain if I have the right information, the information the reader needs to learn, in the right order, and the order in which the reader should learn it.

Once I am confident that I have a logical flow to my chapters, I can begin to outline each one.

What I am asking you to do before you begin to create your detailed chapter outlines is to review your linear work and clustering and come up with the broad strokes — the number of chapters you need and titles for each chapter. This information will anchor your outlines.

Do it now and then come back and take a closer look at a detailed chapter outline.

Sample Chapter Outline

Now, let's look at an outline for one of the chapters of *The Business of Freelance Writing*. I hope you will see how having a detailed outline in place provides structure, gives you a road map, helps you detect errors in logic and helps you write in manageable chunks with greater clarity.

Here is a condensed version of my outline (some of the topic points have been removed) from Chapter 11.

Querying Editors: Overview:

1. Selling ideas to editors — overview
   a. It's like selling any product or service (use examples)
   b. Freelance writers have difficulty with sales and marketing
2. Bottom line: Marketing is important…
3. Define query letter; relate to sales letter
   a. Query letter and follow up are sales and marketing tools
4. Target Marketing
   a. Target specific ideas to specific markets (publications)
   b. Vs. generic 'are you looking for writers?' query
5. Two basic approaches to marketing your work
   a. Submitting unsolicited manuscripts (on spec)
   b. Querying (pitching article ideas) by mail or e-mail
      i. You can also pitch by phone
         1. Pros and cons; why I don't recommend phone pitch
6. Query letter as calling card
   a. Chance to sell your idea and prove you can write

b. It's how the business of freelance writing works

c. Concept of Pitch-er Perfect

7. Three reasons for e-mail or mail query
   a. What most editors expect
   b. Many editors will not look at unsolicited manuscripts
      i. Query shorter, easier to read and demonstrates writer's knowledge of the topic and ability to write
   c. Takes work to write an article
      i. Find out if you will be paid to write it first

8. What if you are a new writer or have limited writing experience?
   a. Submit full article? (Problems with doing so)
   b. Or query (reiterate why)

9. Query letter contains?
   a. Article idea: reinforce focus!
   b. Sources/potential sources of information
   c. Why readers (of target publication) want to read article
   d. Why article should be written now (if timely)
   e. Why you should write the article
      i. Paragraph about you
   f. Note: spelling and grammar count

10. The writing
    a. Writing must be tight and creative, not wacky
    b. Idea must command editor's attention
       i. Intrigue or tickle curiosity
       ii. Must seem like something publication's readers would be interested in / benefit from

   iii. Must be credible — and achievable for you (example of something not achievable for many of us)

11. How to send … Channel of Choice

  a. Mail, fax or e-mail

  b. Which is most popular; why

   i. Exceptions to what you want to do; why

   ii. Where to find 'how to send info'

12. If submitting by…

  a. Mail, fax or e-mail — address each method (format, etc.)

   i. Focus on e-mail

    1. Plain text vs. attached files

    2. Reasons for plain text unless guidelines state other

   ii. What about 'clips'

    1. How to send, how many to send

    2. Website with sample articles

   iii. Reference examples of query letters in next chapter and other examples in the last chapter of book

I hope, looking at the above outline, you can see how going through the outline process will get you to the stage where it is all over but the writing.

Once you are at that point, you should see that writing your book, outline point by outline point, in the remaining 30 days is possible. With a bit of expansion, some of the above points become full sentences, some of the topic and sub-topic groups become paragraphs. Some of the sub-topics, with a bit of polish, become sub-headings in the book, which facilitate the reading process.

Work hard on creating a detailed and comprehensive outline. You have a day per chapter to do so; use your time productively.

If the notion of an outline is foreign to you, I hope my examples have helped clarify exactly what an outline is and why it is important. However, if you need a bit more clarity, perhaps this analogy will help.

Think PowerPoint

If you are conducting presentations or do any public speaking, you might be familiar with PowerPoint. To support your talk, you might create a PowerPoint presentation. Each PowerPoint slide contains points you are going to talk about. The points are not your talk. They keep you on track and support your talk. Your talk is like writing. It is based on the points. You talk from point to point. What I am asking you to do here is to create a detailed PowerPoint presentation for each chapter of your book. The points are not your book. They keep you on track and support your writing. It is your job, after you complete the outline, to write from point to point.

For instance, in my Six-Figure Freelancer workshop, a workshop that shows participants how to find, price and manage corporate writing assignments, I have a section — think of it as a chapter — called Develop Your Marketing Plan. I use a PowerPoint slide to

Develop Your Marketing Plan
Five arrows in your marketing quiver
1. Generate repeat business, testimonials and referrals
2. Build and optimize your website
3. Network with friends, relatives and associates, and through various organizations
4. Advertising and promotion
5. Cold calling and direct mail

introduce the section:

Of course each subsequent slide on the five arrows, above, includes detailed points on how to shoot each arrow. Let's look at several aspects of the first point that I cover in the presentation:

I suspect you would be able to see how the above points facilitate my talk — all I have to do is look at them and away my mouth goes.

Before you start writing, produce a logical, detailed outline. When you get to writing, all you will have to do is look at your outline and away your pen will go — or away your fingers will go across the keyboard.

Generate repeat business, testimonials and referrals
1) What is repeat business?
   a) Repeat business and the trust factor
2) Retail concept of repeat business
3) Why generate repeat business?
4) How often to try to generate repeat business
5) Why you need to be proactive
   a) "Won't they call me?"
6) When and how to communicate with previous customers
7) How do you generate repeat business?
   a) [Note: There are five sub-points under this particular topic point; I've removed them for the sake of brevity.]
8) What to say or write when trying to generate repeat business
   a) Examples of e-mail and phone scripts
9) Scheduling repeat business steps in your marketing calendar
10) When do current clients become previous clients?

Time to Go for a Walk

What next? According to my outline points, here is what I am supposed to tell you to do next:

- Complete a chapter outline.
- Walk away from your work.
- Be open to ideas that may occur.
- Return and revise.
- Read out loud.
- Move on to the next chapter's outline.

My Points in Prose

Allow me to write my points in prose. Your goal is to complete one chapter outline at a time. Once you complete a chapter outline, walk away from it. Go for a stroll, ride your bike, have a cup of tea or coffee, take a shower. It's good to get away from your outline. Doing so distracts your mind while allowing your subconscious to mull over what you have written.

Sometimes, your subconscious makes a solid suggestion: "What about this point? What about this sub-point? If you are going to include that point, shouldn't you also include…?" Be open to such ideas.

When I walk away from my outline, I try to keep a pen and pad of paper handy so I can capture such thoughts. I have been known to walk my dog, have an idea pop into my head and use my cell phone to call my voice mail and leave myself a message!

When you get back in front of your computer, review your outline and revise it based on the new ideas — as long as they still seem relevant. Sometimes an idea that seems brilliant when you are away from your computer falls flat when you try to integrate it into your outline.

Once you have revised your outline, read it out loud. Doing so will help you detect errors in logic and points that are not quite complete. Once you have revised an outline again, put it away and move on to outlining the next chapter. But always be open to ideas that may strike at any time. Your outline is not carved in stone; it is in a computer file that can be easily revised.

My next outline point for this section says this:

- Follow the process — outline, walk away, revise, review/revise — chapter by chapter, until the book is completely outlined.

I don't have much more to add. What you have to do now is outline your book, chapter by chapter, until you are done. This should not feel overwhelming. You have 20 working days to do it — one chapter per day.

Go. Outline Your Book.

Work on your chapter by chapter outlines now and come back to this book once you have completed your outlines. I will tell you what to do next. If you want a hint, read the final paragraphs of this chapter.

Remember the freefall and directed freefall exercises that we did? Once you outline your book, I am going to have you put those exercises to work. They really pay off over the last 30 days of the 60-day process. But for now, go outline your book.

Note: As stated earlier, I presume you are familiar with all the material you want to write about and do not have to conduct any other research to outline your book. Occasionally, people tell me that the process of outlining helps them discover they have more research to do. To that I say, "Congratulations." Isn't it great you discovered you have more research to conduct?

After all, you were going to have to do the research anyway if you wanted the book to be as comprehensive and effective as possible. If you need it, take some time off from your 60 days and do the research, and then continue to outline your book.

Now go. Outline.

Chapter 12: Writing: Days 31 to 60

Welcome Back.

At this point, I hope you have a detailed, chapter by chapter book outline in place. If, on the other hand, you have decided to read through this book before implementing any of the hints, tips and strategies, no problem. Some people like to see the full picture before working on various tasks. At the same time, when it comes time to work on your book, do follow the process described here.

For those of you who are on Day 31, let's get on with writing your book!

I am going to suggest you start each writing day with five minutes or so of freefall. Freefall is a great way to clear the mind before you write. There is no need to do a directed freefall as you will be using it to write your book. However, do try to put in five minutes or so of freefalling — a good stretch, so to speak — before writing.

A Word on Editing

At this point, I am not going to tell you how to construct a sentence or give you grammar lessons. This is not that kind of writing book. However, for anyone in need of a refresher, the last chapter covers how to construct sentences and paragraphs. Once you finish writing a solid first draft of your book, you can turn it over to an editor who can correct any grammatical errors and spelling mistakes, also known as typos. On the other hand, if you are a strong editor, you can give it a good editing and proofreading.

If you have followed the process spelled out in this book, you or your editor should not have to make any significant structural changes (as editors often do). Why? Because you have outlined your book in a logical manner, thus eliminating structural errors. That being said, it is possible your editor, friend, associate, family member or anyone else you might ask to give you feedback or to do some editing, will suggest some structural changes.

They might suggest you move around, add to or delete entire sections of your book. Listen to what they have to say. Be open. Take their suggestions under advisement. Review your book with their suggestions in mind.

If the suggestions make sense — if they will improve the flow of your book or the reader's understanding of what you are presenting — make the changes. If you are not convinced the suggested revisions make sense, don't make them. Or, get several other people to read your book and see what they have to say. If most people trip up at the same place or don't quite get a particular concept, then you have some work to do.

Rome Was Not Built in a Day

Just as Rome was not built in a day, great books are generally not written in one pass. However, if you have created a detailed outline and if you have written from outline point to outline point, you will minimize the amount of structural work you have to do to bring your first draft up to speed. But you will still have to do some work, which is understandable, considering the breadth, depth and length of books.

In short, if you go back to the beginning of this book, you will see that writing is a process and editing is an important part of the process. The planning and organizing spelled out here can facilitate the writing and help minimize the editing; however, every writer needs to learn how to self-edit, or ideally get some editing help.

Writers get so close to their work that they sometimes cannot see the forest for the trees. They cannot see the little things that may not work because they are too close to their work. After writing this book, I gave it to five members of the Professional Writers Association of Canada (www.pwac.ca) to edit and proofread.

Trust me, I listened closely to their sage advice and implemented most of their suggestions. I've been a professional writer for over 25 years and I am not afraid of, in fact I relish second opinions.

Why am I talking about editing, when this section is on writing your book? I could say, "Because my outline told me to do so." But let me give you a more serious answer.

Many neophyte and experienced writers edit as they write. They get the writing and editing process lines crossed and confused. They manage to finish writing — taking longer than they should have taken — only to discover they need to edit the darn thing again, which is an inefficient way of writing. Mixing the editing process in with the writing process also often produces less effective writing.

I want you to understand that you will have to edit your book or find someone to do it for you, no matter what. Editing is a natural part of the writing process. Save the editing for last, for when you have finished a solid first draft of your book, which is what you are going to start to do now.

On With the Writing

What I want you to do now is write, not edit. I want you to write the way you write when you do your directed freefalls.

Look at your detailed outline and what do you see? You see a whole lot of opening lines.

What do you have when you do a directed freefall? An opening line.

I want you to treat each point in your outline as an opening line and use it to direct your writing. As you complete your thoughts on the point you are writing about, you will come to your next directed freefall opening line. Use the line to get you writing about the next point.

Think of yourself as Tarzan swinging through the jungle from vine to vine. Each vine represents the opening line of a directed freefall. As you write, you swing from opening line to opening line. There is no reason to stop until you complete a chapter!

If the thought of writing an entire chapter in one sitting freaks you out just a tad, don't worry. If you get tired, have to go to the washroom or run out of time, it's not a big deal. The rest of the chapter is there, in outline form, waiting for you to come back to it.

Freefall madly from outline point to outline point. If you complete a section of a chapter and need a break, take a break. But don't be intimidated by the thought of writing a chapter in one sitting.

It can be done.

Remember how I had you count the words of your freefalls and directed freefalls? How many words did you produce while writing for 10 minutes or so? Remember how we did the math? We proved you could write your book in a couple of days, so it is possible, with a detailed outline in place, to write a chapter in a couple of hours — as you swing from vine to vine or as you write from outline point to outline point.

Think about it. If a chapter has 3,000 words and you write 200 words in 10 minutes, then it will take you 2.5 hours to get down a first draft of a chapter, provided you have a detailed outline to follow. If you've allocate three or four hours of writing time per day, you will even have some time left over.

What do you do with the extra time?

Here's the Plan

First, before you write a chapter, review the outline one more time. I am not asking you to review all of your chapter outlines, just the one you are going to work on. Once again, make sure the points flow in a logical manner. Ask yourself if any points are missing or if there are any redundant points. Revise as required. This should not take too long.

Once that is done, crack your knuckles and get ready to write from point to point.

You can write until you complete the first draft of the chapter.

At the same time, I am not naïve. I know sometimes, as we write, other thoughts manage to float to the surface. We discover points we could have included. So pause to include them.

We discover some points suddenly feel out of place, as if they belong in another chapter. Pause to move them.

We might find the chapter moving in a different direction for unexpected reasons. Go with the flow. If it really makes sense, look at the points that you are not covering and determine if they should be covered later in the chapter, moved or deleted. Cover them later, move them or delete them.

If you feel the need to take a break before you complete a chapter, finish writing a section (a topic point and its related sub-points) before you do so. Once you complete a section, quickly review the remainder of your outline. Add or shift any points, as may be required. Take your break. When refreshed, resume writing from point to point. Repeat as often as necessary until you complete the chapter.

At the same time, you may also find yourself able to write from point to point without adding, deleting or moving any points. If so, write from point to point and complete your chapter.

This process should take two to four hours, depending on the length of the chapter. Some of you will finish it in less time. Some of you might take a bit more time. But if you apply the process as I've spelled it out here, you will write a 15- to 30-chapter book over the next 30 days. You can do it. If you dedicate time in a disciplined manner, you will do it. You will turn your desire into reality.

More Research Required?

As stated earlier, I presume you are familiar with all the material you want to write about and you do not have to conduct any other research before writing your book. Occasionally, people tell me they discover there is more research to be done when they start to write. If this happens to you, take a break from this process and complete your research.

Once you have completed your research, review your outline to see what impact the new research will have on it. Revise the outline as required and resume writing.

If your outline is detailed enough and structured in a logical manner, and if you have no more research to do, you can write your entire book, chapter by chapter, without pausing to conduct additional research.

But I Just Have to Edit

If you find it difficult to move forward until you have looked back, so to speak, then feel free to finish a chapter and give it a quick edit before moving on. You are still following the writing process: outline, write, edit. After all, you have completed a chapter, a self-contained unit, so there is nothing wrong with doing a quick edit on the chapter for overall structure and content. However, don't get bogged down in placing every comma in the right place. Save the proofreading for the end.

Again, if your outline was detailed and logical, then structure and content should not be an issue. But I know the process of writing can, on occasion, reveal a structural weakness or missing content. Do a quick edit if it helps you get a solid first draft of your chapter in place. You are not mucking up the writing process — you are not crossing the writing and editing lines. You are editing a completed section, a chapter of your book, which is different than writing a sentence or paragraph and reworking it to death before you move on.

Once you write your first chapter, and give it a quick edit if desired, move on. Write the next chapter. And the next. And the next. And the next….

Ready to Write?

Are you ready to write? Or should I say, "Are you ready to freefall?" Are you ready to make like Tarzan, swinging from vine to vine through the jungle? Or in your case, are you ready to write from outline point to outline point through your book?

The only thing that might prevent you from acting like Tarzan the Writer is a weak, incomplete or poorly structured outline. Again, if need be, take some time to review your outline before you write. Get it to the point where you can see and say, "It's all over but the writing."

Once you are there, swing, baby, swing! Write from point to point. Write one chapter after another. Write your darn book.

If you feel you need some writing assistance before you begin, read the last chapter of this book. It deals with how to construct effective sentences and paragraphs. If you are an experienced writer, the section may be redundant. If you have limited experience with writing or feel your writing skills could use some brushing up, read the last chapter now and then start to write your book.

The Process Works

All it takes now to complete a solid first draft of your book is time and effort.

If you have time and you apply the effort over the next 30 days, you will complete a solid first draft of your book. You will be ready to edit and proofread or to hire an editor. You will be ready to get feedback from a few people you know and trust. You will be ready to start thinking about finding an agent or publisher, or to start thinking about self-publishing.

With that final point in mind, the next chapter provides you with information on Lulu.com and several other print-on-demand (POD) companies.

I use Lulu to self-publish many of my books and reports and I am happy with the results. There are other POD companies out there and many small press publishers, like Five Rivers Chapmanry (the publisher of this book) which are using POD effectively to set up publishing companies. I mention several POD companies towards the end of this book and encourage you to shop around and make the best possible self-publishing, or publishing, decision based on your particular needs.

Final Comments on Process

Many non-fiction books start with an introduction. Just because it is called an introduction does not mean you have to write it first. Finish a solid draft of your book, outline the points you want to make in your introduction and write it.

In most cases, there is no need to go over a page or two at most. After all, it is simply introducing potential readers or those who have just bought the book to what the book is all about, kind of like a synopsis or executive summary of a report.

Once you finish the first draft of your book, give yourself some time off. Put it in a drawer for a week before you start to edit it. Once you finish editing (feel the book is structurally sound and covers all the ground you had intended to cover), proofread it to ensure your writing at the sentence level is powerful and correct.

Finally, when you've polished the book to the best of your ability, have several people read it and comment on it.

Take what they say under advisement. Revise as may be warranted, conduct a final proofread and look for an agent or publisher. If you are going to self-publish, I highly recommend hiring a professional editor to give it one last go-over, to catch those insidious little errors that plague us all — even me, even me. In fact, if I don't leave at least one typo behind, I'm shocked!

With typos in mind, here are a few revision and editing tips:

- Spell-check your document, but do so knowing that there are limitations to what spell-check and grammar-check will find.
- Print and read. Your eyes catch mistakes on paper they might miss on the computer screen.
- Read out loud. If it's awkward to read, it's awkwardly written.
- Share your document and ask for feedback. Let people know what you want to hear: Did they understand the concepts presented? Did you provide enough, or too much, information on each topic? Did the book unfold in a logical manner? Was the writing clear and concise?
- Edit and proofread in the morning, if possible, when you are fresh — even if it takes several cups of coffee to get you feeling fresh.

If you are interested in self-publishing, read the next chapter. Read the final chapter if you want to brush up on your writing skills at the sentence and paragraph level.

Finally, if you are looking for an editor to give your book the once-over, feel free to e-mail me and ask for a quote — info@paullima.com.

All the best with your writing!

Chapter 13: A Tale of Self-Publishing

Could traditional book publishers be heading the way of traditional music companies, which are heading the way of dinosaurs, thanks to the Internet? They could, but for different reasons.

For one, people are not endangering the publishing industry by downloading books for free over the Internet, the way pirated music downloading continues to mushroom. However, many authors are eschewing traditional publishers and book retailers in favour of online print-on-demand (POD) companies.

I am one of the many. Although this book is published through a traditional publisher, Five Rivers Chapmanry, my publisher uses a POD company to print the book. However, unlike most self-published authors, Five Rivers works with book distributors to get the books it publishes into online retailers like Amazon and Chapters and to make the book available to retail outlets.

When I first approached a traditional Canadian publisher with my how-to book about freelance writing, I received tentative interest. The publisher wanted to know if I could guarantee 2,000 sales. If so, the publisher was willing to print 4,000 copies and put the other 2,000 into circulation. This was not a vanity publisher. It was a legitimate publisher of popular fiction and non-fiction titles.

I could not guarantee the sales and was not willing to buy that many books to flog at my seminars. So I approached another publisher. By the time the second publisher replied, I had discovered Lulu.com, an online POD company.

Just as the rock group Radiohead is selling its latest CD from its website — cutting out music companies, distributors and retailers — literally tens of thousands of self-published authors have cut out the middlemen and now sell self-published books online. Lulu.com says it has 1.2 million registered users and receives about 4,000 pieces of new content each month. The site says it logs monthly traffic of more than three million unique visitors.

This book was originally self-published using POD. It did so well that Lorina Stephens, a partner in Five Rivers, and I discussed putting it into wider circulation. However, Five Rivers is using POD to print the book, saving on onerous up-front printing fees.

How POD Works

Lulu allows authors to upload books to its website, gives them a storefront address to sell from (such as www.lulu.com/paullima) and processes credit card orders. Lulu ships the books or makes Adobe PDF files available for downloading — depending on what the buyer wants. The PDFs arrive instantly, without shipping charges. Hard-copy books are printed on demand and shipped to the buyer.

Lulu sets the printing fee based on the number of pages. The author sets the retail price. Lulu takes a small percentage of the difference between the printing fee and the retail price and the author keeps the rest (known as the royalty). If I sell no books, I earn no revenue, nor does Lulu. But I also never pay Lulu a cent unless I buy copies of my books. When I buy copies of my books, I pay the printing price, a small mark-up and shipping.

As with Lulu, the POD company CreateSpace does not charge authors an up-front fee to get their books online. In addition, both

Lulu and CreateSpace provide inventory-free, physical distribution of CDs and DVDs, as well as video downloads.

Most other online POD or self-publishing companies, such as Trafford Publishing, AuthorHouse and iUniverse, charge an up-front fee for setting up the book for publishing. This fee generally runs from $1,000 to $2,500. However, other POD companies also give authors advice on how to format books. Some even help create book covers or offer editorial thoughts.

Trafford, AuthorHouse and iUniverse also place books by self-published authors with distributors, Amazon.com and other online retailers. This is a service Lulu now offers for a fee. However, I have opted not to pay for it because I drive traffic to my Lulu bookstore through my website

You can also use the POD company Lightning Source Inc. (LSI) to put your book into the Ingram book distribution catalogue and into the hands of online retailers. Many small presses, such as Five Rivers, are now using it. Having said that, you need to know more about book layout and design when you use LSI than you do when you use many other POD companies. But if you are a totally do-it-yourself kind of person, LSI might be your best option.

If a self-published Lulu author purchases the distribution package, it guarantees listing in many online catalogues (not Chapters in Canada). However, that does not guarantee sales. Whether authors choose distribution channels or not, marketing remains their responsibility.

It's not just authors who see a future in the on-demand universe. Recognizing there is a buck to be made in the self-publishing business, Amazon.com, the world's largest online book retailer, acquired the POD publishing company BookSurge in 2005. I guess Amazon decided that if it could make money from readers it could make money from writers too. In fact, other POD companies have accused Amazon of predatory practices and the issue is now before the courts. You know when an issue is before the courts then somebody somewhere believes they can make money!

The question on the minds of most self-published authors is this: Can I sell my books? As of December 2008, I have sold almost 1,000 books through Lulu. In addition, sales are trending up (most book sales trend down shortly after the initial launch euphoria) and I have two more books in the works.

I will continue to write, create, upload and promote my books – including this one – from my website and on various book-oriented e-mail lists. I am not a famous author, but I am making money and I like the feeling of independence that self-publishing through POD and publishing this book with a POD publisher has given me.

Without the backing of a so-called "legitimate" publisher, I now sell my copywriting book to two university continuing education departments. My *Everything You Wanted To Know About Freelance Writing...* book is being sold by another university continuing education department. My how-to book on writing media releases has been picked up by a do-it-yourself public relations website. And my book on optimizing websites to boost search engine results is selling briskly to small businesses.

With Lulu's business model, I am running a virtual mail-order book business — but I don't process payments, ship books, or keep a basement full of inventory.

Although it costs me nothing to sell books through Lulu, I did have to format my books and design my covers. (Five Rivers designed the cover for this book and did the internal layout.) I have some facility with Word and with a graphics program, so I was able to produce clean layouts and create functional covers. However, creating layouts and book covers could be onerous for some authors, so they might be better off with a POD company that provides such services or at least find a third party to prepare their books for publishing on Lulu.

Now, let's be honest. Most writers who self-publish will not be successful, certainly not *in Harry Potter* or *The Da Vinci Code* terms, or even in terms of Canadian bestsellers (about 5,000 books).

Most self-published fiction authors and poets publish for family and friends. They have no need for publishers or retailers; POD serves them well. However, many non-fiction authors sell books from websites or to complement workshops. The chances of someone wandering into a Chapters looking for one of our books is slim. We have discovered POD can be a very profitable niche.

With a little help from the web and online POD companies, the public is served and the profits that the publishers and retailers would make go into our pockets instead.

At the same time, I am not saying you should eschew mainstream publishers. If you can land a solid deal with a publisher, or can find an agent to negotiate a publishing deal for you, go for it. But if you have a website and don't mind doing some self-promotion, or you conduct workshops or give speeches and are looking to sell books at your events, then do consider POD.

Chapter 14: Sentences and Paragraphs

Those of you who may need some help writing clear and concise sentences and effectively structuring paragraphs will find this quick primer on writing sentences and paragraphs of interest. If you want to spend more time improving your writing, consider buying *Harness the Business Writing Process* (available mid-2009). You can read more information online at www.paullima.com/books or email the author at info@paullima.com.

Active versus Passive Voice

When it comes to sentences, writers should be aware of several elements. One of the most important is voice. There are two voices — the passive voice and the active voice. I promise I am not going to get all grammatical on you; however, I have to use three grammatical terms — subject, object and verb.

In the active voice, the subject acts upon the object. The action is described by the verb. As in: The dog bit the boy.

"The dog" is the subject, "bit" is the verb and "the boy" is the object. In the passive voice, the sentence starts with the object receiving the action, so this form is much more indirect, as in: The boy was bitten by the dog.

Notice the active voice is more dynamic. Also, it takes fewer words to write a sentence using the active voice. This leads to another important aspect of writing: generally, concise writing is easier to read and more easily understood.

Often, a passive sentence doesn't even contain a subject so the person or thing responsible for the action isn't even mentioned. This is why politicians and lawyers often use the passive voice.

Passive voice is not grammatically incorrect. It isn't very concise, however, and can be vague or confusing. Consider the following:

Passive: You were asked by me to submit your expense report by the middle of the month.

Active: I asked you to submit your expense report by the middle of the month.

Passive: Your payment was received two days late by us, which caused delays.

Active I: We received your payment two days late, which caused delays.

Active II: You sent the payment two days late, which caused delays.

Make sure your grammar checker is set up to detect the passive voice. When grammar checker stops at a passive sentence, ask yourself if using active voice would improve it. You don't have to convert all passive voice sentences to active voice. However, make a conscious choice to convert or leave them.

Speaking of sentences, a complete sentence requires a subject and a verb (action): "I laughed."

"I" is the subject. "Laughed" is the verb. But two-word sentences don't always cut it in business writing. So that's when we add the third component — the object: The boy kicked the ball. "The boy" is our subject (the person who does the action). "Kicked" is the verb or action. "The ball" is our object; it receives the action. I call these three elements — subject, verb and object — the heart of the sentence.

If you ever feel that your sentences are getting too complex, find the heart. Once you have identified the heart, you can expand your sentence logically, while keeping the meaning clear.

For instance, where did the ball go when the boy kicked it?

The boy kicked the ball through the window.

What happened to the window?

The boy kicked the ball through the window, which shattered into a thousand pieces.

Tell me more about this boy and the ball that he kicks:

The tall, thin Caucasian boy kicked the blue soccer ball through the window, which shattered into a thousand pieces.

Our sentence is becoming longer and more complex, yet it is easy to understand because we are building around the heart of the sentence. Now imagine this action was committed by a criminal and the homeowners had an alarm system.

The tall, thin, armed and dangerous Caucasian boy kicked the blue soccer ball through the window, which shattered into a thousand pieces and caused the alarm to sound, notifying the security company, which dispatched its agents to the scene of the crime.

Writing Concisely

You can pack a lot into a sentence if you identify the heart and build around it. However, just because you can pack a lot into a sentence does not mean you should. This can make your sentence long, convoluted and confusing. In addition, if all your sentences were constructed in a similar manner, your writing could become a tad tedious to read.

So vary the voice and length of your sentences. However, be aware of wordy writing. Wordy writing sacrifices readability and coherence (passive voice can contribute to wordiness). Your goal is to write concise sentences that clearly convey the meaning that you intend them to convey. In other words, write concisely, but not at the expense of meaning.

To write concisely, please consider removing unnecessary, extraneous, redundant and repetitive words, phrases, clauses and sentences, without sacrificing appropriate detail.

Of course, if the sentence were written concisely, it would read:

To write concisely, remove unnecessary words, phrases, clauses and sentences, without sacrificing appropriate detail.

Notice how we removed the please and consider and changed removing to remove. There may be times in your writing when you want to be less direct to encourage the reader to consider various options. However, if you are a subject expert and if something should be done in a particular way to be effective, say so and remove the qualifiers, such as "please" and "consider" — as we have done in the second version of the sentence. It is not impolite to write bluntly.

And hey, if the reader does not want to do what you suggest, the reader does not have to do it!

It is, on the other hand, possible to be too concise. Think about this version of the sentence:

To write concisely, remove unnecessary words, without sacrificing appropriate detail.

One might argue it is redundant to use "words, phrases, clauses and sentences". However, each is a different part of speech and you may want to identify each one of them because concise writing doesn't just mean removing unnecessary words. Sometimes it requires you to remove phrases, clauses, entire sentences and perhaps even the occasional paragraph.

In short, when giving instruction, be as specific as possible so the reader understands you. Remember, your readers are not a homogeneous mass. Some might get what you mean right away; others might need a bit more information. If you remove all the unnecessary, extraneous, redundant and repetitive information, you can include a tad more appropriate information that some readers might need, without sacrificing conciseness.

In other words, don't write like the bureaucrat would write:

We are less than pleased due to the fact that it is, at this point in time, the season of winter.

Instead, write like Shakespeare:

"Now is the winter of our discontent." — Richard III

At the same time, you don't have to be Shakespeare to be an effective writer. You just have to be clear and concise.

How to Structure a Paragraph

Being clear and concise doesn't just apply to sentences. It also applies to paragraphs. Paragraphs perform three main functions:

- Develop the unit of thought stated in the paragraph's topic sentence, which states the paragraph's main idea.
- Provide a logical break in material, which signals a new aspect of the topic or a new topic.
- Create a visual break on the page, which makes the document easier to read.

You can put your topic sentence at the beginning of the paragraph, as in this example:

The cost of training *new Customer Service Representatives is significant. The organization must cover the price of classroom facilities, instructors, manuals and employee salaries during the three-week training period.*

Notice the topic is: "The cost of training". You could replace "of training" with "of printing documents" or "of heating the office" or any other significant cost the reader needs to know about. In this instance, the topic is "the cost of training new Customer Service Representatives".

You can, on occasion, place your topic sentence at the end of the paragraph. Doing so varies your writing style. It also lets you build up to the topic sentence with a bit of dramatic flourish. This can be effective, as long as it is not overused. Here is an example, with the topic sentence in bold at the end:

Energy does more than make our lives more comfortable and convenient. It enables us to prosper. The proof? The surest and quickest way to reverse economic progress would be to cut off the nation's oil resources. The country would plummet into the abyss of economic ruin. **In short, our economy is energy-based.**

In the above paragraph, we have dramatically built up to our topic sentence. This can be quite effective. However, if you do this too often your writing will become tedious.

One final comment about paragraphs. Look for opportunities to use bullet points or numbered points. Used properly, bullets or numbers let you convey an idea in a manner that is easier for your readers to scan, read and understand. If they are overused, they can make your document look like it lacks focus or emphasis.

Here is an example of a sentence that would benefit from a numbered list:

To start juggling, you must first pick up "A" in your right hand, then you should pick up "B" in your left hand, and then you should toss "A" and then "B" into the air, catching "A" as you toss "B" and catching "B" as you toss "A." Repeat continuously.

Let's see it as a list:

To start juggling:

1. *Pick up "A" in your right hand;*

2. *Pick up "B" in your left hand;*
3. *Toss "A" into the air;*
4. *Toss "B" into the air while catching "A";*
5. *Toss "A" back into the air while catching "B";*
6. *Repeat continuously.*

After reading the numbered list, you know how to juggle. Well, not quite. However, the instructions are easier to follow because your eye pauses at the end of each point so you better understand the steps involved in juggling.

Imagine if we were going to make five recommendations on how to increase the return on investment (ROI) for training new Customer Service Representatives. We would use normal paragraphs leading up to our ROI recommendations paragraph. However, our ROI paragraph would be easier to scan, read and ponder if we used numbered bullets, as in:

To increase the ROI for training new Customer Service Representatives, the committee proposes the following five recommendations be implemented within three months:

1. *Recommendation one …*
2. *Recommendation two …*
3. *Recommendation three …*
4. *Recommendation four …*
5. *Recommendation five …*

Again, don't over use the use of bullets or numbers. But look for opportunities to use them, as I have done throughout this book, to make your writing easier to:

- Scan.
- Read.
- Ponder.
- Act on.

All the best with your writing and your book!

Note: Find out more about the author and his other books on the following page.

About the Author

Based in Toronto, Ontario (Canada), Paul Lima (www.paullima.com) has worked as a professional writer and writing and communications instructor for over 25 years. He has run a successful freelance writing, copywriting, corporate communications, business writing and media relations training business since 1988.

For corporate clients: Paul writes news releases, case studies, copy for direct-response brochures, sales letters, advertisements and other material.

For newspapers and magazines: Paul writes about small business and technology issues. His articles have appeared in the Globe and Mail, Toronto Star, National Post, Backbone, Profit, CBC.ca and many other publications.

Qualified educator: Paul presents seminars on business and media release writing, interview preparation, search engine optimization and freelance writing.

An English major from York University and a member of the Professional Writers Association of Canada, Paul has worked as an advertising copywriter, continuing education manager and magazine editor.

Paul is the author of 8 books and 3 short e-reports:

Everything You Wanted to Know About Freelance Writing…

The Six-Figure Freelancer: How to Find, Price and Manage Corporate Writing Assignments

Business of Freelance Writing: How to Develop Article Ideas and Sell Them to Newspapers and Magazines\

Copywriting That Works: Bright ideas to Help You Inform, Persuade, Motivate and Sell!

How to Write Media Releases to Promote Your Business, Organization or Event

Do you Know Where Your Website Ranks? How to Optimize Your Website for the Best Possible Search Engine Results

Build A Better Business Foundation: Create a Business Vision, Write a Business Plan, Produce a Marketing Plan.

If You Don't Know Where You are Going, How are You Going to Get There? Business Vision Short eReport

Building Your Business Plan and Your Marketing Plan: A Step-By-Step Guide to Planning & Promoting Your Business Short eReport

Put Time On Your Side: Time Management Short eReport.

Available through www.paullima.com/books

Printed in the United Kingdom by
Lightning Source UK Ltd., Milton Keynes
138005UK00002B/217/P